Cover Design and Photo: Skip Moen

Door panel of the Baptistry
Duomo Santa Maria del Fiore
Florence, Italy

Skip Moen, D. Phil.

Guardian Angel

*What You Must Know about
God's Design for Women*

Abridged Edition

"The hallmark of an authentic evangelicalism is not the uncritical repetition of old traditions but the willingness to submit every tradition, however ancient, to fresh biblical scrutiny and, if necessary, reform."

John Stott

Dedication

This book is dedicated to my *'ezer kenegdo* – Rosanne.

By the time you have finished reading this book, you will be quite familiar with these Hebrew words – *'ezer kenegdo* – usually translated "suitable helper". Unfortunately, the English translation obscures more than it reveals. Once you understand the complexity in God's design for a woman, you will need to make some major changes in your view of marriage and the role of women in the home and in society. Making those changes is my personal goal as I learn to be married.

As my *'ezer kenegdo*, Rosanne is the one who nourishes and supports me when I am in alignment with the Lord and who opposes and chastises when I am not. She teaches me that my agenda isn't the only agenda, that no one wins when only one wins and that my greatest faults are never hidden from her. But she loves me anyway.

I believe that God designed a wife to be both friend and enemy at the same time. She is *perfectly* equipped for this combined role. In fact, if God is sovereign in our lives, then He knows exactly who we need to grind down our rough edges and mold us for His purposes. The goal of marriage, it seems to me, is to learn how to draw near to our soul mates and, in the process, be polished to perfection for God's use. This is a life-long journey. Since God doesn't make mistakes (in spite of all the mistakes we make), the presence of one who lifts up a husband and also opposes him becomes the real place of personal transformation. "No pain, no gain" say the bodybuilders. The same applies to marriage – and the *'ezer kenegdo* is uniquely equipped to bring about the gains God requires of a husband, even if some of them are quite painful.

When God built the Woman, He saved the best for last. Undoubtedly, every man would agree. Any man who has any sense at all knows that a woman is the best thing that ever happened to him. When God designed Woman as the pinnacle of His work, He did every man an enormous favor. In a committed relationship, God made it possible for a man to discover something that is essential for his very being. The lesson in that discovery is the reason for this book. God made women relationally essential – for men and for a man's relationship to God. As we explore the deeper meanings of the Genesis story, we will uncover something incredibly important about who we are and how we cooperate with each other. God made everything good, wonderful, right and purposeful. That is especially true about women. It's time that we got in line with His design.

Skip Moen
Montverde, 2010

Acknowledgements

Without the help and support of several wonderful people, this book would never have been written. First among those is Cyndee Sullivan who not only provided financial support but also offered her time to proofread and add many useful comments.

Christina Graham follows closely behind with her encouragement, editing and enthusiasm for this project. Thank you, Myrna, for final proofreading and corrections that everyone else missed.

I would also like to acknowledge the efforts of Patrick Sullivan, Jr., John Thorman, Amy Gomes, Cheryl Durham, Lisa and Paul Michalski and the readers of my daily *Today's Word*. These people have become family to me. Their assistance, encouragement and support made the work a joy rather than a burden.

Edwin Garcia deserves special recognition for the translation of *Guardian Angel* into Spanish.

Thank you.

Guardian Angel

TABLE OF CONTENTS

Introduction

Introduction	1
The "Easy" Button	6
Marriage Exams Are Scary	10
A Heritage of Misunderstanding	12

PART I: Understanding the Hebrew Background

Chapter 1: Cracks in the Paradigm

Can't Live With 'Em, Can't Live Without 'Em	17
The Game Plan	20

Chapter 2: Back To The Beginning

A First Time For Everything	23
The Genesis Paradigm	26

Chapter 3: Order and Purpose

Eve's Prologue	36
The Hebrew Picture Frame	39

Chapter 4: Between The Lines

Alone	44
The Parade	46
Crowning Achievement	50

Chapter 5: The Guide

A Helper Indeed	52
The Purpose	59

Chapter 6: Marriage By Design

A Man Shall Forsake	63

Chapter 7: Attack

Desire?	71
Authority	73
Curse	75
Consequence	78
Turning	85
Adam Too	89

Chapter 8: Adam and the Serpent

Naked	93
It's All Her Fault!	98
I Don't Need You Anymore	103
The Need To Be Needed	107

Chapter 9: DNA Default

The Will To Power	111

PART II: Hebrew Thought in the New Testament

Chapter 10: A Hebrew New Testament

Moving Toward Paul	116
Same Song, Second Verse	117

Chapter 11: Rabbi Sha'ul

Paul and the Tanakh   132

Chapter 12: Women in the Community

Silence   135
Priority   138
Deception   139
One Woman Among Many   142
As The Law Says   143
Women of Authority   146

Chapter 13: Marriage

Submission   151
Head of the Home   152
Submission For Husbands   157
Sex In Marriage   161
But I'm Single   163
Applying The Teaching   165

Chapter 14: Aftermath Recovery

Now What?   170
Back To The Garden   172

Application Summary   182

Guardian Angel

INTRODUCTION: Designed to Bless

Every woman knows it's true. Deep inside, every woman knows that she was designed to bless – to be the counselor, guide and boundary-setter for her man. While every woman knows this is true, most women don't know why it's true – and they certainly don't know why their men don't seem to understand that it's true. The intuitive feeling that you were made for something special; that you were designed to guide your chosen partner toward a fuller, richer relationship; that you were made to sail the high seas of spiritual awareness is *not* an accident. **God made you this way!** The problem is that centuries of bad theology, misogyny and misunderstanding have obscured and replaced what you were designed to be.

This book tells you why your intuition is right and what you can do about it. This book helps your man understand that you are not his enemy or his assistant. You are his guide, his protector, his helper and his rescuer. **You are designed to bless him. God made you this way!**

This book will help every husband realize that his wife is uniquely equipped to prosper him – IF he will get out of the way.

When women don't recognize how God designed them – and when men don't allow women to be who God designed them to be – all kinds of nasty things happen. Romance is hindered. Relationships are strained. Children become substitutes – and problems. The Body of the Lord suffers. Marriage ceases to be the living display of covenant fulfillment. Family pathology is too often the direct result of a refusal to allow women to be who they really are. Men don't actually mean to demean but they have been trained for a long, long time to think that they are the designated authority figures. When they make this mistake, they enable dysfunctional disorder without realizing it. It's not their fault. Since Adam and Eve, we have been victims of this upside-down disaster. But we can recover.

The Biblical Hebraic view of women is radically different than the current cultural view. The Genesis account stands in opposition to the usual Christian interpretation and the Hellenized Jewish practice. If we want to recover romance, rekindle respect, reignite real unity and release each other to experience God's plan, we need to take a serious look at the mystery in these opening chapters of the Bible. We need to actually *read* the words instead of assuming we already know the story. In this book, we will carefully look at God's words in this text, and we will discover something amazing.

There is hope. We can stop loving our spouses to *death*, a phrase that reveals quite a bit about our deep pathology concerning relationships. We can love each other to *life*! We will discover there is another way, a way God put in place at the beginning of all human relationships. We can learn to overcome the cultural misogyny and the mistaken hierarchies. With the help of the One who designed it all, we can recapture the passion of the Song of Songs, the power of Proverbs 31 and the truth of Genesis 1 to 3.

My wife is my *'ezer kenegdo*. That means she has a very special and unique role to play in my life – a role designed by God that is both supportive and confrontational. She is the one alongside me and the one who opposes me *at the same time*. There is a very good reason for this. That is why this book isn't just for women. It's for *men* who want to understand why their women are so loving and so exasperating and for *women* who want to understand why their men are so attractive and so resistant.

This book will change your thinking about women. If you're a woman, it will make clear something you may not have understood conceptually but knew in your heart. Most of all, it will help you see what God intended, why He designed it that way and what happens when we either ignore or don't know what He planned. Women will probably find this book reassuring and confirming. Men may find it a little threatening (which is good) and finally freeing (which is really good). Along the way, we will listen to others who have gone through this same transition. Men will discover what lies ahead and how far they have to go to reach the goal of really deep relationships. As men, we are on a path toward a redeemed marriage where we are no longer alone in the world. That path is often very painful but the goal brings intense joy. We pursue this painful journey because we so desperately need joy in our lives. I am one of these men.

My wife intuitively knows that she is my *'ezer kenegdo*. She just doesn't cognitively understand everything that this means. She would never call herself by this odd Hebrew expression. But what she believes in her heart and what she does by nature only confirms that she has *'ezer kenegdo* DNA built into who she is. Most men I know don't understand what a wife is designed to do and why she is designed to do it. That means most men are constantly getting in the way of her built-in identity, creating enormous stress on the relationship. Both spouses know there is something wrong, but they don't seem to be able to find a real solution. The answer is in Genesis. To find it, we need some really deep spiritual education.

Just because I can write about all this doesn't mean that life is wonderful in our house. Learning to let Rosanne be the *'ezer kenegdo* is a painful and difficult process for me. I have to undo most of my Greek-based, post-modern indoctrination about women. I certainly have to rethink what the church has taught for almost two thousand years. But it is worth it because marriage is practice for the wedding feast of the Lamb. It is the human equivalent of the great relationship between a believer and God. It is the closest thing to heaven that we can experience on earth. It is hope in the midst of a broken world. It has to be worth it! There is no place else where I can learn to be reunited with the one I need in order to become myself.

We are going to cover some pretty difficult ground. While I have tried not to be too scholarly in this work, some of the concepts and vocabulary will be very strange. Some of the implications may be difficult to handle. This isn't going to be an easy book to read. But if you want a redeemed marriage, one that moves you in the direction of the Garden of Delight, then stay the course. We'll start at the beginning with a long look at the text of Genesis. That's where we are going to find the clues we need to put this puzzle back together. We have to proceed like linguistic detectives, moving from one passage to another so that we can see how one verse becomes the foundation for the next. We will discover the fundamentals of what God intended in the construction of Woman. Then we will be ready to apply those fundamentals to issues that have plagued marriages for centuries.

Ready?

The "Easy" Button

"Hello. This is "Auto By Phone." How can I help you?"

"Your ad says you fix cars over the phone. Is that right?"

"Yes it is. How can I help?

"My car won't go."

"Tell me what's happening."

"I can hear the engine running, but when I push on the pedal, nothing happens."

"OK. There's a simple solution. Push harder!"

Would you call this company for your auto repairs? I don't think so. When a car breaks down, the solution is usually *not* doing more of the same. In order to fix the problem, we have to understand *why* things aren't working. That usually means inconvenience, effort and change. Most of us just want the simplest way to make things work. We want an "easy" button. But sometimes there is no "easy" button. Sometimes we have to exert real effort to discover why things aren't working. Too often, we just want to push the button that says, "Fix it." When that doesn't work, we usually try to push the button harder. We are like people who get into an elevator, push the button and, when the doors don't close instantly, push the button a few more times. Doing the same thing over and over but expecting different results is one definition of insanity. When it comes to relationships, we all seem just a bit crazy.

Most of us just want the "easy" button marriage. We just want the quick and simple list of behaviors needed to make things work the way we want them to work. However, since we don't understand the basic design of all the parts, we can't fix things when they break down. We just limp along, hoping that things will miraculously fix themselves while we keep pushing the "easy" button. If we are believers, we ask God give us the "easy button" solution through prayer. Unfortunately, we don't get easy solutions because we don't really know what's wrong. It's time to try a different approach. It's time to understand how God put it all together and what we did to mess it up.

The world changed in 1962. Most of us never noticed the revolution that took place. Thomas Kuhn wrote a book called *The Structure of Scientific Revolutions*. In that book, he demonstrated that science does *not* proceed in systematic, logical ways. We don't get better and better theories about the universe by collecting more and more facts. Science moves forward by *paradigm shifts*. One way of looking at the world is replaced by another way of looking at the world in a kind of "religious conversion." A paradigm shift revolutionizes our way of seeing the world.

The new paradigm doesn't just change our theory. It changes what we call "facts." It changes *how* we see things. Einstein's theory didn't improve Newton's. It discarded Newton's theory and replaces it with something entirely different. Before Einstein, some things in the world were "at rest." After Einstein, the world was different. Nothing was at rest.

Between paradigm shifts, life proceeds on the basis of *incremental* adjustments. In other words, human beings keep trying to make all those little annoying anomalies *fit* the current theory. They try to fit all the square pegs into the round holes. But sometimes the pegs just don't fit. When that happens, ordinary thinking just tries harder. We try to *make* them fit. The more resistance we encounter, the more things begin to come apart – until someone comes along and says, "Wait. Let's look at the world a *different* way." Revolution! Everything changes.

I believe that we are at the beginning of a revolution. It is the *spiritual* re-orientation of the whole world. It is a dramatic, gut-wrenching, mind-blowing shake up. It is scary *and* tantalizing. The ground is moving. The old footholds are crumbling and our past methods are collapsing. We need to stop pushing the same button hoping that something will change.

Reading this book will help you understand the way marriage is *supposed* to work according to the biblical standard. It is a peek at the original design, based on the Genesis account. Because it is about the original, perfect design, this study is also about the *goal* of marriage today. Therefore, it's theoretical at the beginning (since none of us live in Eden) and it's theoretical at the end (when we finally live according to the design). But this book is not a book about how to fix the present state of *your* marriage. It is not a practical guide for a better marriage or a "ten steps to bliss" kind of manual. Instead of telling you what I think you should do (who am I to know that?), this book describes God's view of the ideal, the mess we made of it, and the opportunity to recover from that mess. Of course, *if you know what God intended, you have a chance at aiming for the right goal.* So, in that sense, this book points you in the right direction. But it can't give you the simple steps to get there. There are no *universal* steps, suitable for everyone. We are all at different places along this dusty road and how we take the next step will depend on understanding how far we are from the original and what we *individually* need to do about it. I believe most of us don't really understand the original design. Consequently, we end up trying one marriage formula after another without much lasting improvement. We need to start over.

We can't investigate God's design for marriage without considering His design for women. Every wife is first a woman. Marriage is the *central* relationship that exhibits the designed purpose of a woman. Marriage comes *after* we understand the fundamental design, a design that equips women to do what God intended. If we don't understand the fundamental design of Woman, we cannot hope to fix any of the misapplications and mistakes in the relationship between a woman and a man. If we get married without understanding this design, we are like those people who try to start a stalled car by continuing to pump the gas pedal and turning the ignition key. A flooded car requires air. We have to do exactly the opposite of our instinct. We have to push the pedal down and *keep it there* so the engine can breathe. To have a great marriage, we also have to do things that are the opposite of our instincts – like letting go of control instead of working harder at keeping it. All these actions come from understanding the *design* first. In this culture, there is enormous pressure to rush to a solution *before* we ask the fundamental questions. When it comes to marriage, the fundamental question is not "Do you take this person." It is "Who are you?" So, this book starts with God's answer to the question, "Who are you?" Who are you as a woman? Who are you as a man? Then, who are you as husband and wife?

Because this study looks deeply into the role God designed for women, it touches on much more than marriage. Before husband and wife, there was male and female. The biblical record puts a very high priority on women; a much higher priority than the current religious culture admits. God's design for the female gender of the human species has long been overlooked, ignored or dismissed. Whether or not a woman becomes a wife, the engineered design built into being female uniquely equips every woman as the comforter, the nourisher, the spiritual guide, the challenger, the one who confronts and the one who sets the boundaries. In other words, every woman is described by the Hebrew terms *'ezer kenegdo*. Understanding the scope and depth of this design will be liberating to all women, especially to wives. Understanding this divinely designed role will allow men, especially husbands, to change their behavior and release the power of the *'ezer kenegdo* – a power that was intended to provide prosperity, blessing and the deepest intimacy this side of heaven.

Marriage Books Are Scary

Books about marriage and women scare men. When we discover that the Bible empowers women, men fear dominance. They react to this empowerment by resisting change. In our society, men have been so beaten up over their "failures" as husbands and fathers that they are not likely to warm to the possibility that the Bible portrays women as spiritual guides. The history of the Church and the history of empires convince men that they need to be in charge. So a book like this one could be seen as a threat.

But the *full* picture of the biblical revelation isn't a threat to men or women. Yes, women are empowered. They are uniquely, divinely designed to play a significant role in protection, direction and correction. But dominance is not part of the picture. In the biblical model, *no one dominates*! Each operates *interdependently*. One without the other diminishes the image of God in the world.

Women may read these pages and rejoice. At last they will discover the Bible not only supports their intuitions about being nourishers, protectors, guides and boundary-setters, it *establishes* these roles. This is way women are made! All of those theological restrictions are wrong. They are misapplied and misunderstood cultural anachronisms. God designed women as servant-priests, as covenant bearers and as perfect partners. But as soon as women realize the full scope of their design, they may be tempted to assert this newfound freedom in tragic ways. Women are the *capstone* of God's creation because they are empowered to *serve* their husbands. Ah, you've heard that before, right? But you've never heard what "serve" means from a Hebrew perspective. The husband is the direct beneficiary of the *relationship between a wife and God*. Just as the husband can have no second agenda when it comes to the priority of his wife, so a wife can have no second agenda when it comes to the care and blessing of her husband.

Of course, empowered to serve does not mean being a slave or an assistant. It means bearing the covenant promise of unity. It means directing the marriage toward reunion at every level. It means actions that overcome being alone or enabling loneliness. These concepts are difficult to understand in the Greek-based culture of individualism and independent isolation. That's why we need this book. As you read, don't be frightened. There is nothing here to support a power trip for either gender. We are intended to become what we were designed to be – restored unity.

A Heritage of Misunderstanding

When it comes to theology, we need enough ammunition to defend ourselves but not enough to start a war.

The real tragedy occurs when philosophical, cultural and theological mistakes are used to support the idea that women are restricted in their roles within the body, are subservient to men and are denied their intended design in marriage. Of course, some very well known theologians argue that the Bible says women must follow these Scriptural guidelines. They quote Pauline passages confirming limitations on the role of women within the congregation. They cite Genesis 3 as the basis for male headship. They explain Jesus choice of twelve *men* as proof that women play a "behind the scenes" role. For two thousand years the church has endorsed this kind of subtle misogyny. I believe these conclusions are mistaken. This mistake has little to do with the overwhelming evidence that women are capable, dedicated and passionate about participating in the Body. This mistake is the result of the fact that the church's traditional interpretation of the text has been skewed by its long history of anti-Semitism and its separation from Jewish roots. Because we do not read Paul (Sha'ul) or Peter (Kefa) or even Jesus (Yeshua) from the perspective of first century Jewish rabbinic theology, we strip away the deep cultural framework from the words they spoke. We read them as if they were "Christian", as if their thought patterns are the same ones we have embraced after eighteen centuries of Greek influence in church theology. We interpret their words as if they shared the same worldview we have unconsciously accepted – a worldview diametrically opposed to the Hebraic mindset of the Bible. We think there are really *two* Bibles; the Old Testament for the Jews and the New Testament for Christians, a document written by Christian converts from Judaism with an entirely different worldview than the one found in the Old Testament. Popular Christianity seems to believe that the "church" was created by Christ and refined by Paul.

But this view is wrong!

Every author of the New Testament was either Jewish or a proselyte to Judaism. Every thought pattern, every cultural influence, every word of the New Testament exhibits a Jewish worldview. Yeshua (Jesus) was a Jew! He was not a "Christian" in any sense of the term as we understand it today. Neither were His disciples. They were all God-fearing, Torah-observant Jews who believed Yeshua was the Jewish Messiah. There were tens of thousands of Messianic Jews and gentile believers by the end of the first century and none of them thought of themselves as "Christian."

Why do we investigate the Hebrew words behind our New Testament orientation? We investigate because we need to understand the thought forms, the culture and the insights that represent the foundation of the Biblical text so we can understand what the authors said and *why* they said it. Why is this important for a book about the design and role of women in marriage, the Body and society? If we want to recover what Paul and Peter and John and James, and even Jesus, have to say about the role of women within the Body, we must first understand the Jewish perspective on the role of women in the community and the synagogue. This Hebrew worldview, not an analysis of the *Greek* text of the New Testament, is the proper background. The Greek New Testament is simply an expression of the thoughts of these Jewish men; thoughts steeped in Jewish culture and Torah observance. It is useless to explain Paul's concept of submission if I do not include Paul's understanding of the term from the Torah. Paul does *not* break ranks with his religious heritage. He describes himself, long after his Damascus road experience, as a Pharisee of the Pharisees. He does not say he *used to be* a Pharisee but now he is a Christian. He says he *is* a Pharisee – and a believer in the Jewish Messiah Yeshua. Unless we understand Paul's view of women *from the perspective of a Torah-observant, rabbinic, Messianic Pharisee*, we cannot hope to understand what he says in his letters to congregations of Messianic believers. We must begin *at the beginning*, in Genesis where all Torah thinking begins. Only after we understand what the Torah says about women will we be able to understand what Paul says about women. Only after we thoroughly understand God's original design will we be able to see God's *redemptive* purpose for women (and men) in the Body. To start anywhere else is to start in the middle of the book.

Marriage rests on a foundation. That foundation is the design and role assignments for women and men. Before Genesis 2:24, God describes the creation of both male and female. He assigns them mutual and interdependent roles. Then He provides the paradigm of marriage. Therefore, any biblical treatment of marriage must begin with a serious analysis of the foundation. Before we can understand who we are as husbands and wives, we have to know who we are as male and female.

Back to the beginning!

PART I

Understanding the Hebrew Background

CHAPTER 1: Cracks in the Paradigm

Can't Live With 'Em, Can't live Without 'Em: Marriage in a Fallen World

"Man is incomplete until he is married. Then he is finished." Internet joke.

Marriage doesn't seem to work very well. For centuries, divorce was virtually treated as one of the mortal sins. The Roman Catholic tradition, and its interpretation of biblical texts, left the world with millions of unhappy unions, held together by fear and façade rather than by any genuine love and commitment. That traditional view was not diminished when Martin Luther cut the ties with Rome. Even today considerable difficulties accompany divorced members of the church, impacting their participation in the ecclesiastical hierarchy and sometimes their full acceptance in the community. The stigma of divorce continues. But divorce is not the real problem. The real problem is ignorance about the Scriptural view of marriage and, perhaps even more fundamental, a non-biblical view of the relationship between men and women and the roles and responsibilities of both. *A defective understanding of God's design for women leads directly to broken relationships.* The problem is the *paradigm*, not the relationships. This was true of Adam and Eve and it is no less true of contemporary couples. The Fall had serious side-effects, like reading those labels on modern pharmaceuticals that say, "May cause death." The straight-jacket Christian paradigm cannot account for the striking anomalies observed in *real* women in the world nor for the implications of the Bible itself.

Here's the bottom line:

Men: We can't live with them because we don't understand how women are designed and equipped in God's plan, but we know we can't really live without them because there is something very wrong about being alone. Somehow the appeal for deeper relationship keeps us coming back even if we have no clue about the proper working methodology of relationships. So, we try to make it up as we go, adding a portion of psychology to emotional frustration and spiritual guilt. We know the real aching desire to find that one true woman who will heal our deepest hurts. But because we don't know how God designed her in the first place, we fumble and bumble and stumble, hoping against hope that we will somehow enter the Promised Land before the end of days. We keep pushing the "easy" button, waiting for something to change.

Women: We fight every day to exhibit our natural capacity for nourishing, caring, protecting and supporting our husbands, in spite of the fact that they generally resist our attempts to steer them in the right direction. We know that deep inside we were made to invisibly direct and orchestrate, without looking for credit but with great satisfaction in the results. But those we love the most seem incapable of allowing us to blossom, not because they don't love us but because they don't *trust* us. Our husbands have agendas of their own – and they aren't convinced we really have their best interests at heart. Admittedly, sometimes we don't. But there is something about who we are as women that must find its fulfillment in this nurturing-caring-protecting behavior. Too often, far too often, we turn our energies to our children. As a result, we end up with relationships of mutual toleration with our husbands. We want more but we don't know how to get it. We keep trying the same things – and we get the same results. We want to throw away the "easy" button but we're afraid there isn't anything else.

Of course, there are exceptions to the rule. Once in awhile we run across those couples that seem to have an amazing syncopation. They remain individuals with their own sense of identity, but below the surface they are really one being, inextricably united in thought, word and deed. We are fortunate to have these living models among us, but too often even they can't tell us *how* it all works. Somehow, it just does. We watch in awe, admiration, envy and puzzlement, not knowing exactly what to do to mimic their success, only hoping that being in close proximity will heal our own struggles.

The fact that so many couples seek marriage encounter groups, marriage improvement conferences and dozens of "How To Have A Better Marriage" books and videos is only testimony to the deep and abiding discrepancy between our hopes for a perfect union and the reality of perceived needs left unmet. After the honeymoon, marriages seem to be an inevitable prolonged state of mutual co-existence based on a "too-tired–to-fight" truce rather than an exciting and fulfilling union. We know there must be something more. We feel it in our bones. But in spite of all the techniques, counseling and pundits on the subject, marriage is still a struggle. Sometimes it seems like the work needed for a close relationship is just *too* hard.

The Bible has some advice about all this. Of course it would. It is God's instruction manual for living; and since marriage is at the heart of God's desire for the closest possible human relationship, marriage plays a prominent role in Scripture. It is used over and over as the present physical manifestation of our ultimate relationship union – with God Himself. We can turn to the Bible for the greatest wisdom on the subject. Who knows better than God how this is all supposed to work – even in this broken world?

The Game Plan

I believe the Bible is God's authorized instruction manual for life. But there's a problem. Most of us don't really know what Scripture teaches. Oh, we think we do. We've heard the stories and the sermons, but we've never actually *examined* the text. How are we going to understand the Scriptural view of the creation and role of men and women unless we pay very close attention to the Biblical development of the theme? This means we cannot begin to understand what Paul has to say unless we first understand the Scripture Paul uses to support his arguments. And since Paul was a Pharisee and Torah scholar (the top of his class), this also means we must at least become reasonably proficient Torah readers. Without Torah clarity, we can't hope to see what Paul is saying and why he is saying it. Paul doesn't see the world the way we do. He is Semitic, Hebrew and Jewish. We have tried for centuries to force his thought into Greek, Western and Christian boxes and it doesn't work.

Therefore, we can't begin with Paul. We will begin at the beginning, when God created Man, male and female. We will move slowly through the text, examining each thought for clues about what God intended for the roles of men and women, why certain words in Hebrew are crucial to understanding those roles and how this understanding is supported by other patterns in the Tanakh. Only after all that can we open Sha'ul's letters with any hope of reading his words with Hebrew eyes.

Here's the game plan. It is really a linguistic detective story. We begin with the Genesis account. Genesis sets the stage for all that God reveals to us about who we are and who He is. There is a temptation here to open the scene with the creation of the woman. If we did, we would notice that the critical verse about the creation of a "helper" really relies on prior verses, pushing us back through the creation story. Once we know what God is saying about the creation of male and female, then we will see what this implies about the "helper." There will be a lot of questions; questions that should have been asked before but were overlooked because we thought we knew the story. Those questions will eventually take us through the account of the serpent and the first sin. Finally, we will arrive at the story of Cain, a story that reveals much more about the failure to become human than it does about the first murder.

Once we have covered the Genesis material, we will find connections to several other important biblical passages. In particular, we will find these "helper" words in Proverbs 31, Song of Solomon and Jeremiah 31. Examining these passages will prepare us to finally turn to Sha'ul. Then we will see *why* Sha'ul says what he says and this will help us understand *what* Sha'ul is really saying.

CHAPTER 2: Back To The Beginning

A First Time For Everything

We celebrate first-time events in life. The first birth of a child, the first word, the first step a child takes, the first day of school, the first job and a host of other "firsts" are all important signs of progress. In language, the first occurrence of a word is often critical for understanding the word. That is the role of etymology – to trace the history of the word back to its beginnings, its first occurrences.

This principle is particularly important in Scripture because we believe, by confession of faith, that these words are not randomly chosen words for story-telling or ethical training. We believe they are the very words God wanted to use to communicate His purpose, character and instructions to men and women. For the believing community, these are *sacred* words. As a result, substituting a word with an *approximate* synonym will never do. The Scriptures tell us we are not to add to or subtract from *any* of these words. Therefore, when we seek to understand the meanings of the words God uses, we better pay very close attention to their first occurrences in the original language. That means we will have to take a serious look at the *Hebrew* text.

When it comes to the design, purpose and role of women, there are first-occurrence words in the biblical creation account that set the stage for everything else. Some of these words will be familiar to us in translation, like "helper" or "help-meet". Some will be relatively unknown, like "desire" and "corresponding". There are two problems with an approach that relies on the translated words. The first is that the translation often hides linguistic clues that show these words are related to each other or to the story in general. Without the Hebrew architecture, a reader never sees the intentional structural connections. In addition, translations often substitute many different words for the same underlying Hebrew word. There are two reasons for this substitution. First, translations tend to follow the grammar and syntax of the translated language. When repetition isn't *stylistically* in good taste in the translated language, the translators often substitute a synonym rather than simply repeating the original word. While this produces a more eloquent translation, it obscures the connections between the words in the original. It preserves the idiom but loses the interconnectivity. Secondly, sometimes the context seems to call for another meaning or nuance. Once again, the translator substitutes a synonym hoping to capture the added meaning. When this happens we no longer see the essential correspondence of the underlying Hebrew words. Hebrew is a sparse and terse language. One Hebrew word may cover a very wide range of meanings. While it isn't *wrong* to use many different words in the translated language to capture the range of the Hebrew word, the essential connections are lost because we don't read it *in Hebrew*. This is truly unfortunate because Hebrew not only shows us the relationship between concepts through the meanings of the words, it also shows us the relationship between the concepts by the *construction* (the actual letters) of the words. When our understanding and application is based on the translation, we are immediately in trouble.

Hebrew is a language written only in consonants. Furthermore, it lacks any punctuation. This means the nuances of the message are often communicated in changes in the *structure* of the text. For example, rearranging the word order often tells us what word is the most important. Sometimes a consonant is doubled in order to add something crucial to a word. Sometimes a word is repeated in another form to add emphasis. And sometimes a word in one sentence is connected to a word in another sentence by repeating the consonant structure so that the reader can find a thought-relationship between the two even if the meanings are different.

The difficulty, of course, is that almost all of these subtle alterations are *lost* in translation. We will try to recover these lost ideas. In ancient times, Hebrew was a pictographic language much like Egyptian hieroglyphics. Word pictures reveal more about the Hebrew thinking behind crucial concepts, but word pictures are never seen in translations. Consequently, we must understand the consonant architecture as well as the etymology in order to grasp the full meaning of the Hebrew text.

You can think of Hebrew like the supporting structure of a building. The steel girders and the concrete foundation hold the whole building together. When the building is complete, you never see the supporting structure. The Hebrew consonant structure of the language is like those girders. Where the girders have the same structure (the same order of consonants), the language *shows* us that these two passages are connected. Unfortunately, you have to *see* the plans in Hebrew to see the relationships. Once the words are translated into another language, the consonant structure disappears from sight.

What application can we take away from this little lesson? We aren't living in the time of Abraham. We might not speak or read Hebrew. But there is a lesson here for us. That lesson is the ability of God's Word to connect one thing to another in ways that we could never anticipate or imagine. Who could have guessed that Abraham's military rescue of Lot, his encounter with Melchizedek and his refusal to take booty from the king of Sodom would be connected to the foundation of God's eternal blessing of Abraham? The Hebrew text shows us that there is a connection – a connection that is obvious *only* in Hebrew, interpreted through Hebrew eyes. When we come to the text about the creation of Woman, we must look for the same sort of structural connections. They are there if we look at the Hebrew architecture. There are first-occurrence words, structurally similar words, doubled words and other connections within the architecture of the language. We will have to look at each of these before we can really understand what the text says about women.

The Genesis Paradigm

Above all else – Order. The first chapters of Genesis provide us with a paradigm. The clarion call of the first word decidedly differentiates the Genesis view from every other cosmology of the ancient world. Few Christian readers appreciate just how radically different this view is, principally because we have almost twenty centuries of re-interpretation of the Hebrew text, read with Western, Greek eyes. But when we examine the *original* text, we find an ordered existence that *defines* the great questions of life within the Hebraic biblical paradigm. One of those questions is "What is the role of the Woman?" "Why was she created and what is she intended to accomplish?" This question is fundamental to any inquiry that touches on the biblical view of women, and in particular, the biblical view of marriage.

God starts at the beginning. One of the very first things that we discover is that God is a God of order. This is an incredibly important point. The account of creation in Genesis differs from every other ancient account of the beginning of the world because in the Genesis account God *creates* order as soon as He begins to speak. There were many competing myths about how the world began. Most of them involved struggles between good and evil or wars among the gods or some other kind of conflict. Many included the domination of one god over another. But not Genesis. It alone distinguishes God from all creation. It alone describes the creative activities as order making events. The common phrase "after its kind" and the references to boundaries set the stage. When God creates, He establishes peaceful harmony and divine design. This pattern is repeated in the creation of human beings.

Genesis 1:26-27 is the first critical passage. It is usually translated, "And God said, "Let us make Man in our image, after our likeness; and let them have dominion over the fish of the sea, and over the birds of the heavens, and over the cattle, and over all the earth, and over every creeping thing that creeps upon the earth. So God created Man in His own image, in the image of God He created him, male and female He created them." As many commentators have noted, the verse establishes the equality of the sexes, assigning dominion to both without distinction. God orders existence so that male and female human beings equally share their assigned, designed tasks. But there is much more here. Humanity bears the image of God. Humanity has one tie to the earth because *adam* is formed from the dust of the ground, but there is another tie. That tie is to God's image and likeness. Exactly what this means is one key to understanding the role of the Woman.

Many theologians have commented about what it means to be made in God's image and likeness. The precise Hebrew words (*tselem* and *demut*) are often used for statue, shadow or form. It's interesting that *tselem* is a masculine noun and *demut* is a feminine noun. Image and likeness seem to incorporate both sexes without qualification. Theologians suggest these two words cover the unique qualities of human beings such as free will, moral awareness, self-consciousness and spirituality. Arguments can be made for all these aspects since they distinguish human beings from animals. However, what we need to recognize is perhaps not quite so philosophical. Hebrew is a phenomenological language. That means it portrays life *the way it appears*. Greek, on the other hand, is an analytic language, attempting to uncover the reality behind the appearance. Furthermore, Hebrew is an action-oriented language, focusing attention of the dynamic flow of life (verbs). Greek is a concept-oriented language focusing on the people, places and things (nouns) that are the subjects of the actions. Consequently, when theologians speak about the essential qualities of human being in terms like free will, morality, self-consciousness and spirituality, they employ terms that really belong to a Greek worldview. These descriptions are *things* – qualities, characteristics and attributes – rather than *actions*. The Hebrew view may be far more relational and event-oriented. What it means to be created in God's image might be much more like what it means to be flowing water than what it means to be a chemical compound of hydrogen and oxygen (H_2O). In other words, the idea of being human just might be about what we *do* rather than how we are constituted.

How do the two Hebrew terms, *demut* (likeness) and *tselem* (image) explain what it means to be human? In Hebrew, being human means acting according to God's path to life. It means standing against chaos. It means participating in a covenant guarantee. It means knowing what is permitted and what is not, and *acting* accordingly. Any behavior that denies, negates or rejects these goals is not human behavior and the creatures that exhibit non-human behavior are not creatures that exhibit God's image. Before sin entered the world, God made human beings as perfect representatives of His image and likeness. Now we discover that this is an *active* and *dynamic* condition. In the perfect creation, nothing prevents human beings from taking on the image and likeness of God. *They are human because they act as God's representatives*. It is a process of dynamic interaction with roles, responsibilities and a relationship with Him. But when sin entered the picture, something tragic occurred. Human beings began to move in another direction. Over time, those who were designed to become human rejected walking this path. They eventually arrive at a destination not intended for human beings. Human beings are intended to arrive at the full expression of "our image and likeness." But it is also possible to arrive at another destination, as we will see.

To be in God's image and likeness is to desire to control or have authority over chaos. That sounds very familiar. The picture reflects the prime directive: to be fruitful, multiply, subdue and steward – all actions that require authority over chaos.

If Genesis is anything, it is the proclamation of God's authority over chaos. Genesis announces the God of order, the God who brings organization and purpose to the formless and void (Genesis 1:2). If human beings have anything in common with the Creator, it is the ability to bring order to chaos and exercise authority over structure. Human beings are "like-ordering" beings. They reflect the divine image when they bring order to life in the house, the place God has provided for them to live. This is the Genesis version of Luke 2:14, "Glory to God in the highest and *peace on earth.*" Peace is not the Greek idea of the absence of war. Peace in Hebrew is *ordered and harmonious existence.* It is harmony within the will of the Father. Our authority is derivative. It depends on God's sovereign authority. But it is authority nonetheless. As long as we are acting as His agents manifesting actions similar to His, we exhibit His image.

This text reveals something crucial about being human. The image of God is not a static element. It is not something that we possess like flesh and blood. It is a dynamic activity. I reflect God's image as the order-maker when I act as the order-taker. It is action within the relationship that constitutes the image. We are manifested as human beings when we act humanly, when we act in ways that manifest the image and likeness of God. We might say with Soren Kierkegaard, "Now, with the help of God, I can become myself." We are in the process of *becoming* human. In the same way that the divine name of God is a verb, the image of God is a verb.

Human beings are order-makers within an ordered structure. That ordered structure surrounds what it means to be "male and female." To be created in God's image is to reflect divine action. We are not human because we have the *capability* of being human. A water bucket has the capability of holding water, but it does not manifest its purpose until it actually contains water. Just so, being human is not the capability of making choices, bringing order to chaos, ruling or creating. To be human is to *act like God acts*, to reflect His choices. It is not to *be* God. It is to be His sons and daughters, and in Hebrew thought, that means to be a reflection of the Father.

When we investigate the Hebrew words for male and female, we discover another layer of the order-making meaning in the process of being human. Male (Hebrew *zakar*) is a noun that appears 82 times in Scripture. It is most likely derived from a root that means, "to be sharp, pointed". It stands in complementary opposition to the Hebrew noun for female (*neqevah*), derived from a verb that means, "to pierce." The sexual metaphors are obvious, but that is not the end of the story.

Zakar has a homophone, another word that is spelled exactly the same way in Hebrew (Zayin-Kaf-Resh) but has a different meaning. As a *verb*, *zakar* suggests some very interesting possible connections to the Genesis creation account. The principle meaning of *zakar* as a verb is "to remember." While we think of remembering as primarily a cognitive process, Hebrew mental activities are intimately connected to actions. In Hebrew, *zakar* describes a presence of mind that is taken to heart. In other words, this cognitive activity is personal relational activity that results in volitional choice. It is *thinking* that becomes *doing*. Hebrew does not make the same distinctions that we find in Greek. A person is not separated into body, mind and soul. In Hebrew, there is only the whole person – the embodied, God-breathed animated being who stands between heaven and earth. There is no better example of this connectivity than the description in Psalm 103:18. The verse reads, "To those who keep His covenant and remember His precepts to do them." The purpose of *zakar* is not simply to bring something to mind. It is to bring something to mind *in order to act upon it.*

Do you see why the homophone of *zakar* is so intriguing? Is it possible that being in God's image as male (*zakar*) could be related to a man's necessity to remember who God is and how God is related to men? Is part of the divine image the activity of *remembering* where I came from, whom I serve and whom I depend on? The homophone of *zakar* suggests that a man is human in the *action* of bringing to mind the necessity of obedience to God and *doing what is required*. This theme can be found throughout Scripture. Man is called to remember – in particular to remember God and his obligation to God, the Creator. In this sense, Adam bears the image of God as the one who is called to remember what God said, who God is and to act accordingly.

There is another indication that remembering is essential to what it means to be a man. Hebrew has two words translated "man." The first, of course, is *adam*.

This word means the individual man, the person Adam, or Mankind depending on the context. There is also the word *ish*, introduced in Genesis 2:23. The introduction of *ish* in Genesis 2:23 is important because it allows a Hebrew word play with the word for woman (*ishshah*). We will turn to this linguistic humor in a moment, but now we must recognize that *ish* also has a homophone, a verbal stem that has two meanings. The first is to show oneself as a man, to be strong. The second is to fix in mind. Once again there is a connection between being a man and remembering. Adam's unique task was the one that made him a male – to remember what God said and do it.

What about "female?" The Hebrew *neqevah* also has another story. The Genesis 1 account unifies *neqevah* (female) and *zakar* (male) in the creation of human beings. What is essential to being human must be found in the combination of *zakar* and *neqevah*. Beyond the obvious necessity of reproduction, the concepts contained in both words are needed for human beings to be human.

Neqevah has its own unique enhancement. In addition to a homophone (discussed below), the Arabic cognate not only means, "to pierce, to make a hole," but also "single out" and "appoint as a leader." These meanings are found in Hebrew Scripture. Could it be that the *neqevah* (female) is *appointed* to an office of distinction, a role that carries a special identity and bears the mark of that identity in her gender?

What about the homophone? *Neqevah* comes from the verb *naqav* (to pierce, to designate, to curse). *Neqevah* is simply the noun derived from this verb, but the verb construction has a homophone, *neqev*, that describes a prepared setting for precious stones (Ezekiel 28:13). In other words, the homophone of "to pierce" means "a purposeful boundary, a designed setting." This may seem incredibly strange to us. There is no apparent connection between "to pierce" and "a designed setting," unless one of the implied associations of the homophone connects a female with a boundary. If *neqevah* is the "pierced one", perhaps the homophone suggests that she is also the "boundary-setter", "the designed setting" for human dynamics. This word may point us toward the complementary roles of the female: appointed to a high office revealing her identity, a conduit for all subsequent name-giving identity and the one who maintains the boundaries.

The roles of male and female, found in the structure of the Hebrew words, fall into line with the subsequent narration. Immediately following God's announcement of the creation of Man as male and female, the text tells us that God blessed them and gave them the divine command to be fruitful, multiply, replenish the earth, subdue it and have dominion over it. The prime directive is mutual, functional, ordering and purposeful. Both genders are entirely involved in the effort and operation. Neither is given hierarchical priority over the other in this divine assignment. Before we examine the deeper structure of the divine prime directive, let's summarize.

The interrelationship of the words suggests the following:

1. To be human is to *act* as a reflector of God's actions. Human being is a verb, not a noun.

2. Both male and female are necessary complements of what it means to be human.
3. Masculine and feminine genders are needed to comprise the entity known as Man.
4. Male and female equally receive the prime directive.
5. No hierarchy of assignment or subordination relationship is implied in the divine command.
6. The male may be connected to the idea of remembering the place of Man, the authority and sovereignty of God and the action obligations that result from remembering.
7. The female is described not only as the one whose very existence supplies a name for all who come after her but also as the one who is specifically designed and equipped for a high office or royal appointment.
8. The female may be connected to the idea of protecting boundaries.

God concludes with the pronouncement that everything He made is very good. He blesses His ordered creation. This is the foundation of all of the detail we will discover in Genesis 2. The big-picture view of Genesis 1 demonstrates that everything is in harmony. We have discovered hidden treasures in image, likeness, male and female. Now we must turn to the details of this order to see how Man and Woman fill in the picture.

Chapter 3: Order And Purpose

Eve's Prologue

Immediately preceding God's statement about the need for a "suitable helper" (an *'ezer kenegdo*, a word combination that will become very important later) is this command:

"Of every tree of the garden you may freely eat, but of the tree of the knowledge of good and evil, you shall not eat of it; for in the day that you eat of it you shall surely die." (Genesis 2:17).

Once again we must understand the complexities of this text if we are going to see how it is connected to the creation of Woman.

Was the commandment only about eating? Think about it. Does that really make any sense? Why would God put so much emphasis on an activity that is essential for life itself? Adam has to eat. That's patently obvious. And whether he eats from this tree or that tree really doesn't make a whole lot of difference, does it? If he is permitted to eat from *any* of the trees except one particular tree, then why make a big deal about eating? Nevertheless, that's what's happening in this particular Hebrew word arrangement. The text reads *achol tochel*. It's really the word *achal* written twice. It's as if God repeated Himself in order to underline the idea. "Adam, I don't want you to just eat to live. You can really *feast* on whatever is here in the garden. Let your eating be a joyous consumption, a celebration of delight. Go for it!"

Do you suppose God was encouraging Adam's gluttony? I doubt it. We need to examine the Hebrew verb *achal* in order to see something beneath the surface. Let's start with the pictograph. Aleph-Kaf-Lamed paints the picture of "the strength to control what is allowed." In other words, this verb for consumption already incorporates the concept of control. It isn't eating until I am stuffed. It's eating for enjoyment and delight. This is not an "all you can eat" buffet. This is a gourmet meal. The act of consuming acknowledges our responsibility to control what God allows. We can feast because He gives us permission, but we are still responsible for *how* we consume.

This picture changes a few things. First, *achal* is no longer just about food. Did you think this story was about apples, pears, peaches and plums? No, it's about *everything God gives* in His place of delight. Remember, *'eden* is God's pleasure palace. He puts *ha'adam* in the place dedicated to everything delightful because He wants the earth-creature (Adam) to experience the doorway to life (the pictograph of *'eden*). Food is only a tiny sliver of all the delightful things God has given. Start thinking of Eden as the place of endless wonder, joy, excitement, awe, pleasure and celebration and you will begin to understand the emphasis on *achal*. Feast on life in the place dedicated to delight.

Here's the best part. Eden is located where God delights to provide pleasure. Eden marks the spot wherever God puts the earth-creature in circumstances that encourage delighting in His gifts. *Achal* is about consumption, not just about eating food. What may we consume? Start your list. How about consuming the beauty of morning skies, the wonder of bird songs, the smell of freshly cut grass, the delicious coolness of a mountain stream, the delight in the smile of a child, the exquisite tenderness in a lover's kiss, the joy of community fellowship, the mystery of God's presence. Did you think Eden was paradise lost? Think again. Man was given permission to feast on whatever God allowed.

God intends us to experience all good things, to enjoy every delight He has prepared whether it is aesthetic, cognitive, emotional, physical or spiritual pleasure. His version of fruit salad extends to every aspect of creation.

What does this mean for us today? It means that God determines what is good. We are placed in His world according to His instructions. If we want real pleasure in life, we will live under His sign – the sign that guarantees control over what is allowed. Sin is determining what is good outside of the boundaries of His covenant.

Adam was assigned the role of prophet, priest and representative of the King. The only reason for the existence of the tree of the knowledge of good and evil is the test of proper judgment. Would Adam faithfully reflect God's determination of what was good and what was evil, or would Adam choose to obey another authority? In other words, the tree is a symbol of the most ancient and most deadly of all sins – idolatry. Surprisingly, the manifestation of the concern about idolatry is found in what to *eat*! The first command is about dietary laws. What sets Adam apart from the rest of animate creation is Adam's willingness to allow God to determine what he will eat and what he won't eat. Adam is not to be driven by his desires. He is to be guided by God's word. He is to remember what God said, and *act accordingly*.

The Hebrew Picture Frame

In order to finish the prologue, we must look at the consequences of disobedience. Our study of the consequences will become critically important when we look at the actual results of the fall in Genesis 3, but for the moment we need to fill in a bit more of the Hebrew structure. This command reveals more than the translation allows. The additional insights help us understand exactly why the next event in the narrative is about the Woman.

Let's look once more at God's instruction to Adam.

"Of every tree of the garden you may freely eat, but of the tree of the knowledge of good and evil, you shall not eat of it; for in the day that you eat of it you shall surely die." (Genesis 2:17).

Hebrew handles emphasis by manipulating the structure of the language. Words are *arranged* in ways that draw attention to particular ideas. The Hebrew words *achol tochel* (eat freely) emphasizes the diversity and sufficiency of God's garden of delight by repeating the root *achal* twice. Doubling the word puts emphasis on the idea. Putting the word in first or last position in the sentence does the same thing. In this verse about the tree of the knowledge of good and evil, another word is doubled. That word is *mot*. The verse in Hebrew doesn't say, "surely die." It says "die die" just like the verse says "eat eat."

Something else is happening with this structural arrangement that we need to know. Hebrew thought is often grouped inside a word frame called an *inclusio*. Hebrew doesn't have paragraphs, so if I want to draw a frame around one particular idea, I must draw the frame with words. A double word in one place draws my attention to a double word in another place. I am encouraged to consider the *similarities* or *differences* between the doubled words in order to understand the full thought of the narrative.

The first doubled word (*achol tochel*) describes the magnificent fecundity of God's delightful provision. Everything I need is present and available to me. Notice that the words used for enjoying God's full provision are *descriptive*. They state the facts about the Garden. It is a place where true satisfaction is found under every tree – except one. In the same "frame," the words about dying are also *descriptive*. Under that one tree, life as defined by God comes to an end. This is a description of the facts, not a *prescription* of ethical behavior. God isn't giving Adam a *rule*. He's telling Adam the way it is. "If you eat of that tree, then this will happen." The parallel double words connect descriptive statements. God doesn't command Adam to eat from every tree. He offers every tree. In the same way, God warns Adam about the one tree. In both cases, God states the *facts*.

Why is it important to notice that the parallelism inside the frame is descriptive rather than prescriptive? It's important because we can't understand the punishment for disobedience if we don't understand the *structure* of the prohibition. God says (descriptively) that eating from this one tree will result in *mot tamoot*. Adam eats. But he doesn't die instantly, does he? He lives for many,

many years. Christian theology accounts for this discrepancy by saying that Adam died *spiritually*. But that doesn't maintain the parallelism. The opposition is between fully satisfied and empty. Feast or famine. Adam's choice is between God's design for delight or his decision to make his own garden. What Adam loses with his choice is a place in God's delightful life. He is thrust out of the Garden into a world of his own making without the delightful provisions of God. As a result of disobedience, he experiences *insufficiency*. He has to labor to find delight. He goes from feast to famine, just as God said he would.

We tend to think that Adam's sin resulted in spiritual separation and spiritual separation results in death. From this, we proceed to the need for repentance and redemption. In other words, we connect Adam's sin with Yeshua's death, placing them both in the *spiritual* arena. Of course, there is a connection between Adam's disobedience and Yeshua's redemption. Sha'ul (Paul) is quite clear about this. But this isn't the *only* consequence. As the concluding element of the frame, *mot tamoot* describes what it means to be outside of God's delight. It isn't just spiritual death. It's alienation from the provision of God. Adam's sin turns delight into destitution. To live under God's umbrella is to experience His provision. To disobey is to experience emptiness and struggle. There's more to death than spiritual eventualities. In fact, from a Hebrew perspective, the *eventual* spiritual condition isn't nearly as important as the present reality. Unlike Christianity, Hebrew thought is primarily focused on this world. What matters most is being in God's will *today*!

What follows this warning? What follows the only prohibition God gives Adam? The need for a "suitable helper", the *'ezer kenegdo*. The argument proceeds from the prohibition concerning the tree of the knowledge of good and evil to the requirement for a helper. Furthermore, the entire story of the first sin focuses on the role of the *'ezer kenegdo* and the tree. How can we ignore the obvious conclusion that the purpose of the *'ezer kenegdo* is somehow connected to the command for Adam to obey? Adam doesn't need an assistant or a co-laborer. The assignment to care for the garden, be fruitful, multiply and take stewardship over the earth is given to *both* male and female. They equally receive God's prime directive. But the command prohibiting eating of the tree of the knowledge of good and evil is given to Adam alone. It is not Adam's productive energy that needs assistance. It is his faithfulness to God's instruction. He needs a *protector, encourager and spiritual director*. He needs someone assigned to keep him on the straight and narrow. He needs one who comes alongside for the express purpose of guiding his obedience.

Eve (Havvah) has a role to play, but it is not the role of domestic companion, production assistant or Vice President for Public Works. Unless we recognize this aspect of the description about the Tree, we will not acknowledge that her role is the role of *priest and spiritual guide* for Adam! She is designed to make sure Adam stays faithful to God. She is the one who stands between God's command and Adam's obedience, watching over him so that he will not go astray. Adam guards the Garden. Eve guards Adam. The help she brings is the help of reminding, rescuing and demonstrating trust. In this role, she parallels God's ultimate relationship with Israel. God is the protector, provider and deliverer of Israel in the fallen world, but those are roles God takes upon Himself *after* the Fall. In order to understand the role of the *'ezer kenegdo*, we must look at God's relationship with human beings *before* the Fall.

CHAPTER 4: Between The Lines

Alone

Now we can leave the prologue and examine the story itself. It begins with being alone. Why did God construct (the verb means to build according to a plan) this woman? The text tells us God saw it was not good for the man to be alone. But wait a minute! Adam wasn't alone. He had the companionship of all the other creatures. The Talmud suggests that Adam's relationship with the animals was very deep and intimate. Certainly if we can experience loving relationships with animals, Adam knew this sort of encounter even more than we. After all, he lived in a perfect world. What more could He have needed? You might suggest what he really needed was a "personal" relationship with someone like himself. But he had that too. He had an unblemished, untainted relationship with *God*. How could anything more be needed? Isn't it enough to have a personal, face-to-face relationship with the Creator in a perfect world?

Apparently it's not. Adam might not have realized something was missing, but God did. It is God who recognizes that the situation is not good. This pronouncement stands in stark contrast to everything else in creation. God acknowledges every other part of creation is good. He blesses His work. But when it comes to His last effort, He sees something incomplete. In some way, Man is alone, and this is not good. Both words are crucial for understanding of what this means – for Adam and for us.

Now we are doing some serious digging. We will have to keep moving *backwards* through the text in order to see why Woman enters the picture at this precise moment. To do that, we will have to know how the Torah connects all the previous information to this decision to provide a "helper".

We need to know what it means to be alone. The Hebrew word is *levado*. The root is *vad*, but here it has an attached particle *le*. *Vad* has two meanings. They are distinguished by the particle attached to the root. When *min* is attached, the meaning is "apart from" or "besides" (see Exodus 12:37). But with *le*, the meaning is "alone" or "by itself." God says it is not *good* for man to be by himself. Actually, the Hebrew text uses the verb *hayah*. In light of many other passages, we could translate this "it is never good for man to *be manifested* by himself." In other words, the full sense of what it means to be human will not be revealed until this creature is manifest in some way that exhibits both male and female. One without the other means something vital is missing. The meaning of "alone" in this text is tied to what we have already discovered about the secrets of carrying God's image and likeness and about the secrets of being male and female. To be alone is to be without the complement necessary for becoming human. It is to be a *single actor* in a world where image is defined by *community relationship*. The male, the one who remembers, still requires another, a boundary-setter in order to properly bring about the order-making activity of God's image. To know what to do is not enough. Man must also know how to do what he is supposed to do and know where to do it.

Being alone is a symbolic representation of disorder. Something about the way Adam is supposed to be manifested requires more than his individual existence. Behind this is the Hebrew idea that Man is not a collection of individual biological entities. Man is manifested in community. You and I are not (never) alone. We are constituted as "us." We exist *together*. Any other arrangement is "not good" because it does not represent the order of the universe. Creating good is the principle *action* of God's design. This Hebraic paradigm shift is especially important when we consider the formation of the *'ezer kenegdo*. The term God uses for the woman is not simply a description. Hebrew views reality in terms of actions or purposes. So *'ezer kenegdo* is a manifestation of a *purpose*. The Woman isn't described by the terms *'ezer kenegdo*. She is the purpose inherent within *'ezer kenegdo*. This is what she *is*, just as God is a shield – the manifestation of rescue and protection.

The Parade

God knew Adam needed this partner before He paraded the animals in front of Adam. God always knew there would have to be a "helper". That's why the creation account in the first chapter of Genesis provides the summary remark, "created them male and female." There was never any doubt that H̲avvah (Eve)[1] was an essential part of creation. So, why does Adam need the parade?

---

[1] The Hebrew name of the woman given to her by Adam is Chet-Vav-Vav-Hey (*h̲avvah*). This name in Hebrew has implications that cannot be derived from the English substitute "Eve." "Eve" is neither a translation nor a transliteration of the Hebrew name.

We could suggest the parade was simply an educational lesson. God knew, but Adam didn't. Adam had to discover for himself that there was no *'ezer kenegdo* for him. This is a lot more than discovering there is no "helper" among the animals. Actually, there are a lot of helpers in the animal kingdom. For centuries, animals were the quintessential helpers of men, only recently replaced by their mechanical substitutes. Clearly the idea of "helper" in the sense of assistant laborer doesn't fit the text. Adam did not lack conversational companionship, psychological interaction or purpose. What was it that Adam had to discover that could not be provided among the animals *and* could not be found in a relationship with the Creator? Why was it necessary for Adam to discover this fact on his own? Why didn't God just build Havvah and present her as His gift?

These are difficult and dangerous questions. They are difficult because they force us to reconsider the familiar story. This time we actually have to *read* what it says. They are dangerous because they call into question many of our preconceived notions about the Eden experience.

Adam needs to recognize on his own that no creature *under his authority* is suitable for him. Because the rest of the animals were placed under Adam's authority through the symbolism of naming, he must discover there is no *subservient* creature that fills the requirement. This implies that Havvah is *not* part of the order under Adam's authority. When she arrives on the scene, she is not beneath him. She comes as an equal. He does *not* call the shots for her. She is not part of the animal kingdom. She is exactly equal to him. That's why Adam exclaims, "This one is flesh of my flesh and bone of my bone." In other words, for the first time he finds a being that is exactly like him.

Of course, this is what God had in mind from the beginning. There is no suggestion of a hierarchy of authority in this perfect balance. Remember this when you read those difficult passages in Sha'ul's letters. Sha'ul is a Hebrew Torah scholar. What he says about the man as the head (Greek – *kephale*) of the woman must be consistent with the Torah's description of this relationship. Since these words in Torah are the basis of Sha'ul's argument, we must know precisely what the Torah says. The text tells us H̲avvah is *not* built *under* Adam's authority. Even Adam acknowledges her equality following their sin. She is taken *from* him to emphasize the fact that her very substance is *equal* with him.

The fact that H̲avvah is not a part of the animal kingdom is important for two reasons. First, she and Adam are unique. The difference between human beings and animals is so important in the biblical text that it cannot be overemphasized. The world proclaims we are merely a higher evolution of animal, not distinctly different in origin or essence. The Bible has a very different perspective. The Bible doesn't debate the proposed theory of evolution. That simply isn't important from a biblical point of view. What is important is the deliberate connection between Man and God. There is no doubt about our connection with the rest of creation. We are made of the same stuff as the earth. But notice that God forms Man from the ground, not from the animal chain. God animates His earthly creation with His own breath. Man is the only created being with a built-in bond between heaven and earth. To be human is to recognize, nourish and exhibit this dual relationship.

Havvah's origin from Adam sets the stage for the biblical view of human sexuality. The Bible says that Man was created male and female. While it is obvious that gender is part of the animal order, the Bible *emphasizes* gender when it comes to human beings. Why? Why not just say (like the animals) that Man was created after its kind? The Bible specifies the gender of Man for two reasons. First, sex is sacred. It is not like the reproductive instinct of the animals. Human sexuality has a spiritual component, a component that elevates it above mere reproductive capacity. It is possible to ignore this component and act like animals, but that is not the way we were created. There is something special about the sexuality of human beings, something that can't be captured in a "how to" manual. The creative element of sexual reproduction will become an important consideration when we see what happens to Havvah *after* the first sin.

Nahum Sarna points out that human sexuality is on a completely different order than sexuality among the animals. It is a *gift* from God. Properly understood and properly enacted, it cannot be anything but spiritual and good. God made it that way. Sarna explains this is the reason that sexual perversion is so offensive to God. Perversion is corruption of the very nature of Man, a degradation of God's breath in our human form. Nevertheless, as important as this is, it is *not* the focus of the creation of Woman.

Crowning Achievement

There is one other factor that must be recognized from the text. Havvah is the *last* of God's creations. Sarna notes there are no other ancient creation stories that include the creation of the first woman. Hebrew is unique in this. Furthermore, the Hebrew text gives *priority* to the woman's creation, spending six times more textual detail on this event than on the creation of the man. The origin of woman is the capstone of all God's work, signaling that the entire plan is now complete. It is the most important event in the whole story, positioned last to signify its emphatic climax. It is the finishing work, without which the Painter/Composer leaves something vital undone. From a Hebrew perspective, Havvah, not Adam, is the concluding masterpiece.

When Adam (the person) announces the female will be called Woman, there is a word play in Hebrew that we don't see in translation. For the first time, in this verse, the word used for "man" is *ish*. When the man (*ish*) announces the word "woman" for the first time, he uses the Hebrew word *ish-sha*. You will see the phonetic similarity. Woman comes out of man. The text uses a Hebrew word play when the man says, "She shall be called woman because she was *taken out of* man." Adam recognizes her essential equality and unique similarity in his choice of word. The point is emphasized in the Hebrew text because *ishshah* is *not* a derivative of *ish*. Etymologically the two words are unrelated. Therefore, the word play is deliberate and intended to make the point that the two are uniquely equal.

With the word *ish-shah*, Adam acknowledges the dangerous bliss resident in this perfectly suited partner. This recognition is crucial for Adam. Adam says, "She shall be called Woman" for she is his own identity now released from within him, standing before him in support and confrontation. This is free will personified. Man can no longer do whatever he wishes. His freedom must be worked out within community.

As we will see, God's description of the female as *'ezer kenegdo* is much deeper than Adam's description in the word *ishshah*. The two are clearly connected. Both words seem to support the underlying concept of one who complements and opposes. The biblical record is not some kind of worship of Woman. It's not pagan Mother Earth and it's not the idolization of Mary. It is simply the biblical recognition that God chose women to be the way that every living human being becomes a member of the working-worshipping community. It's not idolatry. It's the recognition of something vital. Mothers matter!

CHAPTER 5: The Guide

A Helper Indeed

Then the LORD God said, "It is not good for man to be alone; I will make him a helper suitable for him." Genesis 2:18

We start with the Hebrew words used to describe this creature God is about to construct. "I will make for him a helper" is the usual translation of the second part of the verse. The Hebrew text reads: *lo-tov heyot ha'adam levado e'ese-lo 'ezer kenegdo*. The critical phrase is *'ezer kenegdo* – "a helper corresponding to". The meaning of this phrase is extremely important.

Linguistic detective work in Hebrew immediately tells us something unusual is happening. *'ezer* is not the word that we would have expected. It is found in Genesis 2:18 and 20, and never again in the book of Genesis. Furthermore, God chose the word *'ezer* to describe the woman. It wasn't Adam's word, *ishshah*, or Adam's name, Havvah, nor does this text repeat the previous word for female, *neqevah*. By the time Adam gets around to giving the woman a name, all kinds of drastic things have happened. The name Adam provides is Havvah. As we will see, this name hints at her post-fall identity in more than one way.

God's choice of *'ezer* is quite an unusual one. First, the word is masculine. We recognize immediately that something strange is happening here. The gender locus of this word must come from someplace else.

'ezer shows up in other texts in the Scripture.[2] In about half of the seventeen occurrences, *'ezer* is used to describe God's relationship to Israel. Let's start with the divine characteristics of *'ezer*. What functions does God perform as the *'ezer* of Israel?

Exodus 18:4 – God *delivers* from the hand of the oppressor. He *rescues* from danger.

Deuteronomy 33:7 – God *assists, supports and reinforces* Israel against her enemies.

Psalm 33:20 – God is Israel's shield, *delivering* Israel from death and showering Israel with lovingkindness (*hesed* – a much bigger concept than this single word can convey).

Psalm 70:5 – God *provides* in times of affliction and need.

Psalm 115:9 – God is the one that Israel must *trust* (see also Psalm 115:11).

Psalm 146:5 – When God is *'ezer*, Israel is *blessed* and has hope.

God is the *'ezer* of His chosen people. This is quite significant since it supplies a whole list of actions that are characteristic of *'ezer*. These actions, seen in the

---

[2] *'ezer* occurs once in Exodus (18:4), twice in Deuteronomy (33:7 and 26:29), less than a dozen times in the Psalms, and once in Isaiah (30:5), Ezekiel (12:14), Daniel (11:34) and Hosea (13:9). There are six additional occurrences where *'ezer* is part of the proper name of a person. One is an Ephraimite, two are priests, one is a builder, one is a Judaite and one is part of the company of David's mighty men.

relationship between God and Israel, help us understand what role the woman plays as *'ezer* and why it is appropriate for her to be called by the masculine noun *'ezer*. This word carries the idea of help from one who is *more capable*. In fact, the etymology of this word suggests someone who has superior military strength. That, of course, is precisely the implication when the word is used to describe God's relationship to Israel. But it is hardly what we have come to imagine about the role of the "helpmate" in our contemporary society.

'ezer isn't a common word in Scripture. It's not the word for "wife" or the typical word for "woman". Perhaps God's choice of this word is another indicator of the capstone of His creative majesty. He not only makes a person through whom an entire species of voluntary worshippers will exist, He also positions her as the final statement of the divine image manifested in the flesh. To be the *'ezer*, she is to play the same role with her man as God plays with His people. That includes deliverance from oppressors, rescue from danger, assistance, support and reinforcement, shielding from death, blessing within a covenant relationship, provision in difficult times, trustworthiness, hope and forgiveness. No wonder she is the capstone of creation.

'ezer is derived from the verb *'azar*. The noun *'azara* is also derived from this verb. It means "enclosure," a particularly interesting nuance of the Semitic idea of help. The various expressions from the root word include military aid, social and moral support, deliverance, salvation, enclosure (protection) and general assistance. What is most revealing is this: God is always the assumed source of true help. For this reason, the noun *'ezer* is often used to describe the

character of God. He is the *helper* par excellence. *Azar* means "to rescue or save or to excuse." The general sense is military assistance. In contrast to the false gods of idolatry, it is God's nature to help. You don't have to convince Him, appease Him, placate Him or prove your worthiness in order for Him to act on your behalf. Aside from the fact that false gods are *false*, the distinctive difference between YHWH and idols is this: God helps *in spite of our unworthiness*. God showered His love on us when we were still acting as His enemies. He helps when we least deserve it.

The foundation of help after the Fall is forgiveness. It is simply inconceivable that God should help those who stand in opposition to His sovereignty, holiness and majesty unless He *forgives*. Help comes because God forgives. Those who avail themselves of His generosity are the ones who recognize this. It is only on this basis that we, the unworthy, can cry out, "*Azrenu!*" ("Help us!"). When the Genesis account tells us that God chose the word *'ezer* to describe His purposeful construction of the woman, the connections to His own actions are deliberate.

One etymological root of *'azar* is Sabaic, a language of Old South Arabia. In this language, the root consonants (Aleph-Zayin-Resh) mean, "to ask forgiveness." This is also related to an etymological root that means, "to cause oneself to be helped." Let's connect the dots. God desires to help. To ask for His help is, at the same time, to ask for forgiveness. In that action, we are causing help to come upon us. When we take even the tiniest step toward the Father, He jumps to our aid. This background helps us understand Yeshua's parable of the Father's passionate rush to meet the wayward son.

This raises some immediate questions. Does this mean that God designed the woman to carry out actions typical of His own character? Is she the provider, protector and priest? How can the *'ezer* exercise forgiveness in a perfect world? What does this imply about her relationship to the man? If the *'ezer* is connected to forgiveness, how does this work if women are sinners just like men? What about Yeshua? Isn't He the *only* one who brings forgiveness? These are all important questions, but the answers will have to wait until we fill in the rest of the picture.

The pictograph adds more to the meaning. *'ezer* is the Hebrew consonants Ayin-Zayin-Resh. These display a picture of "first cut from a person", "to see a weapon of a person", "to experience the weapon of a person" or even "the first weapon (of defense) of the person." The woman is certainly the first cut from the man. In fact, she is taken directly from him. And the role of the *'ezer* is to protect, help, provide and nourish. Certainly this is the biblical view of strength and defense. What God had in mind is not subservience or patriarchal hierarchy. His choice of *'ezer* indicates the woman is a man's first line of defense, an equal partner in the journey of life, equipped for a special function in the life of her mate. The *'ezer* is God's gift to the husband. She is *built* to bless him. She is Adam's protector! Perhaps the biblical account gives much more credence to our saying, "Behind every successful man is a good woman" than we have really understood. In the detailed account of the creation of Adam and the woman, it is the woman who occupies center stage.

In summary, Scripture tells us a woman is God's chosen protector, provider and strength for a man. Secondly, she is from Man, equally a partner under the Lord and perfectly matched for re-union as one. Finally, she is the physical transporter of life for all Mankind. These three roles are all wrapped up in one person. They are separate but united. When we confuse them, when we put all the emphasis on one of the pictures and ignore the other two, we end up with terrible distortions like the pagan Mother Earth or the contemporary idea of woman as servants of men. Scripture reveals all three, intertwined. And a cord of three strands cannot easily be broken.

What does this tell us about the *original* purpose of Havvah? Did God intend Havvah to be the protector and provider, the stronger party, in the male-female relationship? There can be little doubt that these thoughts are implied in the choice of *'ezer*. She is the one who will be his strength, who will safeguard him. But safeguard him from what? More digging is needed.

The Christian world has almost universally misunderstood the concept of *'ezer*. More often than not, the role of the "helper" has been viewed as some kind of assistant, available to carry out delegated tasks not specifically assigned to the male. Household maintenance, child rearing and domestic tasks become the boundaries of the helper's world. With this preconceived status, we ignore those parts of Scripture that describe women in terms other than domestic managers. Even Proverbs 31, often proclaimed as the model of a perfect wife, is reduced to actions under the oversight of the male. Typical English translations of Proverbs 31:10 use words like "excellent" or "virtuous." But the Hebrew word *hayil* is connected with strength, wealth and warrior, not with moral virtues. The shift in translation from "woman of valor" to "woman of virtue" reveals the bias of the translators' culture. As we shall see, Proverbs 31 is heroic poetry, not a simple description of the duties of a good wife. Thousands of years of cultural assumptions do not justify these conclusions. The Biblical record suggests a different picture.

Given the patriarchal history of humanity, we are tempted to think Woman was created as Man's *assistant*. But the Genesis account presents a different picture. Delegation by the male is never included in any part of the original design. Genesis 1:27 includes both male and female in the single category of "our image, and according to our likeness." Both genders are created in the image of God. Both have equal status before God as created beings. How they differ is not a matter of the display of the divine image but rather a matter of what roles they play in the divine drama. Those roles are not built into the way they are created. They are subsequent to their creation.

If *'ezer* is God's word for Woman, then this word should reveal something about her designed purpose. Just as the word *'adam* tells us about the essential purpose of Man (worker of the *'adamah*), so *'ezer* tells us about the purpose of Woman. After all, God didn't just randomly wave His magic wand for her to appear. The Hebrew text tells us that God *crafted* her according to a deliberate and specific plan. The Hebrew verb used in the creation of Havvah is a verb that suggests a carefully constructed, according to plan, designed production.

We have established the woman is not subordinate to man, the woman is the crown jewel of creation and the woman plays a special, deliberately engineered role in the human relational fabric. We must also acknowledge that the procreative function of woman is *not* yet part of the story. The recognition of her life-continuing role comes *after* the Fall. At this point in the text, she is *'ezer kenegdo*, God's words for her identity. When God builds her, her purpose does not arise from her sexuality. This is crucial because it implies that her divinely given purpose *remains* intact even after her role as mother of all living moves to center stage. She is built for a purpose that only she can fulfill. The remaining question is: What is this purpose?

The Purpose

When Scripture uses an odd combination of words to describe something as important as Woman, we better pay attention. Nothing is stranger than the way the Torah describes the creation of Woman. She is called a "helper" *kenegdo*. We have examined the first word, *'ezer* (helper). It absolutely does *not* mean assistant. It's much more like military aid, guide or rescuer. In some sense, so far unidentified, a woman "saves" a man (most men already know this, even if they can't admit it). That, however, is just the beginning. As we discovered, she is designed to *bless* him. Now we need to know *how* she does that.

The Hebrew text doesn't use the word *'ezer* alone. The full concept is *'ezer kenegdo*. Unfortunately, the addition of the word *kenegdo* increases potential confusion. That's because *kenegdo* occurs only once in Scripture, right here. The word is made up of two Hebrew words, *ki* and *neged*. *Neged* is not a noun, a verb or an adjective. It is a preposition. That is very odd indeed. It's like saying H̲avvah is a "helper before" or a "helper in front of". The meaning of this preposition by itself (*neged*) is determined by the context. It covers the range "before, in front of, corresponding to, against and opposite." Even more disturbing is the fact that here the preposition *neged* has been coupled with *ki*, another preposition that usually means "like" or "as." Commentators have struggled with this combination. Clearly the words are critically important for understanding what God intends in His creation of Woman, but many scholars of the Christian tradition tend to either gloss over or ignore this combination of prepositions.

Rabbi Shlomo Riskin provides an essential modification.

> The first problem is the strange Hebrew term, "Ezer kenegdo," the phrase G-d uses to describe the creature He will provide for Adam in order to conquer his being alone. The literal translation is help-opposite. Other translations are "help meet" or "a help to match him" or "compatible helper"; terms which do not fully reflect the inner tension of the concept. Rashi, in explaining the phrase, writes, "if the man is worthy, then his wife will be an 'ezer' (a helper), and if he's unworthy, she'll be a 'kenegdo', (against him, an opposite force)." Despite Rashi's commentary, a help-opposite is still an unusual term. If it's not good for Adam to be alone, why doesn't G-d simply create a 'helper' for him, why an 'opposite'?[3]

---

[3] Rabbi Sholmo Riskin, "Prashat Bereishit: A Help Opposite?" The Florida Jewish News, October, 2003.

This question is the crucial one. Rabbi Shlomo suggests that the answer lies somewhere in the arena of equality. In a very important observation, he says, "Husband is not meant to control wife. If he does, he has lost out on discovering his 'ezer-kenegdo,' and he will never be able to overcome his social loneliness. We cannot partner with a lesser being whom we subdue! (The phrase "he shall control her" is a punishment and a far cry from the ideal)."[4]

Before she was a wife, she was the *'ezer kenegdo*. As *'ezer kenegdo*, she is both advocate and chastiser. She is *perfectly suited* to act as the intimate guide for a man to stay connected to the Lord. And she is *perfectly opposed* when her man is tempted to have his own way. She is able to draw him to her in a way that nothing else can. When she is truly *'ezer kenegdo*, she protects her man as no other. She is his ultimate weapon against unrighteousness, even when that unrighteousness is found within him. She is the boundary-setter, designed with special awareness of God's intentions. The popular idea of a woman's intuition acknowledges that she is equipped with a certain sensitivity that eludes men. She plays a role that he *cannot* play, not simply in procreation but as the one who brings reinforcements, encouragement and sustenance. She is God's representative close at hand. She is *perfect* because God made her that way. She is *perfectly* equipped to fulfill the purpose God had in mind. This is *built into her*. Furthermore, she is the *perfect opposition*, the perfect enemy, when her man steps away from obedience to the Lord. She knows him better than anyone. She is part of him. She is his shield and guide. Therefore, she is perfectly equipped to deflect his excuses, see through

---

[4] Ibid

his justifications and ignore his rationalizations in her effort to align him with his own perfect purpose.

But this glorious responsibility and awesome power comes with a terrifying risk that we must also acknowledge. The story of her design is accompanied by the story of the Fall. Unless we understand why the Woman is at the center of this next chapter, we will not comprehend the terrible power of the *'ezer kenegdo*.

Chapter 6: Marriage By Design

A Man Shall Forsake

Before we turn to the great disaster of the first sin, we need to examine one other connection. The narrator of our story adds this thought immediately following the presentation of the woman:

Therefore, a man shall leave his father and mother, and shall cleave to his wife, and they shall become one flesh. Genesis 2:24

"Therefore" means that as a result of something previously explained, the following happens. Therefore, "therefore" is a very important word in this text. Without it we will not know *why* a man (*ish*) should forsake (that's what it really says) his parents and cling (cleave) to his *ish-sha*. So, let's back up. Adam coins the word "woman" because the woman comes out of the man. She is bone of his bone, flesh of his flesh. Notice he does not say "blood of my blood." That is already established in the creation of Man. Adam sees she is the perfect complement to him, the one he was designed to embrace as his equal under God. She comes from him.

Man and woman are two elements of the same original union. We are to bring about the restoration of that union by an exclusive relationship that reunites the single entity. That is the purpose of marriage. It is not lust abatement, economic cooperation or passionate possession. It is re-union. It is homecoming. It is two becoming one harmony again. This is "soul-partner" language, and it is what we all yearn to find.

The two critical verbs in this ultimate declaration concerning marriage are equally informative. The first is *azav*. It means, "to leave, abandon, forsake or (turn or cut) loose." The consonant picture is the idea of a leader cut off from the house. The second verb is *davaq* (to cling, to cleave, to join with). The pictograph of *davaq* (Dalet-Bet-Qof) shows us a door to a house *behind*. In Hebrew, the *future* is behind us, out of our sight. We can see where we have been, but we are not able to see where we are going. This word is the picture of a new home, one that is in the future, *behind us*. So, these two verbs actually paint the same picture as the word description of the verse itself. A man is cut off from leading in one home and finds a new home in his future. That new home is the place of the *'ezer kenegdo*, the place where he is re-united with his alter-self in union with the one who was made for him.

Perhaps husbands need to spend some time thinking about the biblical view of "one flesh;" a view not based in the Greek overtones of sex. Perhaps husbands need to discover what *they* are missing. Perhaps they need to realize that reunion is the goal of marriage. Then they may choose to become whole again by acknowledging the role of the *'ezer kenegdo*.

If we skip forward several millennia and examine the commentary of Yeshua on this verse, we see the same reunion objective. Consider Matthew 19:6 *"What therefore God has joined together, let no man separate."* Every translation I checked has the same wording, "joined together." But that doesn't quite capture the overtones of this very unusual Greek verb (*syzeugnymi*). The verb literally means, "yoked together." It is found only twice in the LXX (Ezekiel 1:11 and 23). Both are translations of the Hebrew verb *havar*. When Yeshua spoke about the purpose of marriage, he must have used this Hebrew verb. It isn't just about "joining." It's about pulling the load *together*. Joining is what we do with lumber, pipes and committees. But *yoking* implies work to be done. No one hitches two animals with a yoke without having an objective in mind. The point of yoking is pulling in the same direction in order to accomplish the same purpose.

Two people who are *joined* together in an agreement for mutual pleasure, protection and provision are not necessarily *yoked*. To be yoked is to share the same task. This is the purpose of marriage as God sees it. My spouse and I must share in the same God-given objective. Without this, we may be joined but we are not yoked. Of course, that doesn't mean we do the same *job*. We may both have different tasks in the world but we have the same objective. What is that? It is to live in yoked harmony, recapturing what it means to be one again in a display of perfect redemption. Our objective is reuniting. We two are to become one. This language should remind us of Yeshua's prayer in John 17. To become one is the highest of divine objectives. That is the purpose of marriage.

Yoked means pulling *together*, not pulling apart. Yoked means deep friendship, anchored in common commitment. Yoked means *not being alone*. Yoked means holding hands while we travel the path of God's purpose in a broken world. Yoked means not letting go. Lots of couples are married, inside and outside the church. Few are yoked. Those who aren't know they aren't. Those who are can't imagine what it would be like not to be.

The divinely created complementary nature of human beings stands behind the sacrament of marriage. Marriage is the *normal* state of affairs, an essential building block of society, the intended design of the Creator and the right fit for a man and a woman. There are no biblical texts that support any alternative for societal preservation. But this is *not* the reason a man leaves his home of origin and attaches his fidelity to his wife. We noticed the verse begins, "Therefore (*al-ken*)." That means that there is something *before* this thought that entails "leaving and cleaving." What precedes verse 24 is Adam's joyful expression that in the creation of the woman, God has built the absolutely ideal partner for him. Just seeing her leads Adam to proclaim this is almost too good to be true. A man would have to be a fool not to see it. He leaves his childhood home and attaches his fidelity to his wife because God meets his deepest need for companionship in the creation of a woman. The biblical perspective is not that a woman needs a man in order to feel complete. The biblical perspective is the *man* is missing some element of himself before God provides a true and perfect companion.

But now we run into a problem. The verb for this reunion is not *hashaq*, a verb that means adhering to someone in love. The Hebrew word here isn't what we expect. It's not even wedding ceremony language, at least not the kind of weddings that we are used to. This verb is *davaq*. It's about superglue. It's about gluing boards together or making mud pies. It's really not about how I *feel at all.* It's the sticky stuff – the unbreakable commitment of fidelity, loyalty, honor and obedience that comes with the deepest of all human relationships. It's the kind of commitment the Bible describes in Song of Songs: passionate ownership, devoted sacrifice and sensual enjoyment. It's the kind of fidelity we see in Joseph, husband of Mary (and not, by the way, what we see in Abraham). It's the husband of Proverbs 31:29, proudly proclaiming his wife surpasses them all. It's holding on and sticking together like the scales of a crocodile (Job 41:17). It's a picture of the kind of fidelity God shows toward us, and the kind we are to show toward Him. This is *covenant* language.

We once asked how the *'ezer kenegdo* could act as priest and guide in a perfect world. We asked how she could be connected with the idea of forgiveness. Now we see the answer. She has a covenant relationship with God; a covenant relationship that is built right into her very existence. Her connection to the Lord is precisely what equips her to accomplish the purpose of her existence – to bless her man. She is the physical manifestation of God's grace, the one who guards him and guides him toward harmony with the Creator and the creation. She embodies the attributes of the truest *'ezer*.

Unfortunately, for most of us this is merely theoretical. We acknowledge this is what marriage *should* be. This is what God intended, but our reality is squeezed in the vise of the fallen world. We don't have utopian marriages. We have pedestrian ones.

It's a very good thing the Bible is not a book about ethics. It is not a handbook for positive thinking and wonderful living. It's not a Boy Scout manual or a ten-step self-help book. It's a book about *God's point of view*. It's a book about fallen people in a fallen world struggling to live a redeemed existence. It is a hardcore, down-and-dirty story about *God's fidelity* and our screw-ups. Nearly every hero of biblical proportions is, at the core, a tragically fallen person. Without God's intervention, we wouldn't give them a second thought. That is exactly like you and me, especially in marriage. Without God's intervention, our marriages will be little more than frustrating attempts at compromise. Who needs that? We want the joyful proclamation of Adam, "This one is *perfect* for me!" How does that happen? It starts with *davaq*. Sticking to it! Men need to concentrate on the glue! Women can be heroines of Proverbs 31 when men are stuck to them like chewing gum on a cat.

The marriage covenant is consistently portrayed as an example and a symbol of God's covenant with His children. From Deuteronomy to Hosea, the Tanakh uses the relationship of marriage to picture our relationship with God. It is hardly surprising that the design of the *'ezer kenegdo* reflects the covenant faithfulness of God. He is the faithful lover, the one who pursues and the one who cherishes. He reveals the path of well-being and keeps us on course. He insures that we are not alone in the universe.

The Hebrew word *davaq* means more than simply glued together. It implies fidelity and faithfulness. It means holding on over the long run. It's an *unbreakable* word. The word describes God's reliability and consistency fastened to His covenant. In an age when marriage is little more than financial and sexual convenience, it's good to be reminded that God's point of view is not about a workable arrangement but rather about a permanent commitment regardless of the behavior of the other partner.

In the model for marriage, the husband forsakes his father and mother and clings (*davaq*) to his wife. This is certainly not what we expect or what we practice. I would venture to guess that you have never been to a wedding where the bride waited at the altar for the groom to be given away by his parents. Since the biblical model is clearly *not* patriarchal, you might ask how our marriage ceremony developed. What's important is this: a husband is to cling to his wife in the same way that we are to cling to God. There are several other verses in the Bible that portray the same analogy. In each one, God is represented by the woman, not the man. The Woman and YHWH stand on the side of the covenant. The Man is the *beneficiary* on the other side of the covenant.

There are two important implications here. The first is obvious. The quality of my marriage is determined by my long-term fidelity and attachment to my wife. As a husband, I am required to break all other human relationship expectations and shift everything to her. She cannot fulfill her role as *'ezer kenegdo* unless I cling to her. If I am to benefit as husband, I must be glued to her. There is a lot more to this than simply staying together, as we shall see. In precisely the same way, God cannot fulfill the role of the *'ezer* of His children unless they cling to Him. We can easily elaborate the ways we must cling to Him if we are to benefit from the covenant promise. The trick is to apply those same principles in marriage.

Secondly, the comfortable orientation of the culture toward male dominance and patriarchal thinking is not part of the biblical pattern. The role of the *'ezer* is established *before* the first sin. God assumes this role throughout human history. This should give us pause. While feminism seems to be the wrong-headed attempt to replace male dominance with female dominance (and thereby turn women into men), the female orientation in biblical thinking may not be as strange as we first assume. The God who chooses the second when men choose the first may just be the same God who represents His deepest desires for relationship in terms of the divinely designed role of the female, not the male. Feminism is as misguided as male chauvinism. Both attempt to rewrite the biblical design in their own image.

This much is certain: God expects us to cling to Him and to our spouses. If you aren't experiencing this in marriage, how do you expect to make it work with an invisible soul mate?

The *'ezer kenegdo* is designed to play a role analogous to God's role with His chosen ones. But this raises a very thorny question. If this is God's engineered design, then how come virtually the entire history of the world has been operating on the assumption women should be in a supportive or even submissive role to men? How come we seem to have it backwards? The answer requires a closer look at the first sin.

Chapter 7: Attack

Desire?

"And when the woman saw that the tree was good for food, and that it was pleasant to the eyes, and a tree to be desired to make one wise," Genesis 3:6

The critical story about the *'ezer kenegdo* is the story of the Tree of the Knowledge of Good and Evil. It is the story of temptation, but it might not be the kind of temptation we commonly ascribe to this event. The role of the *'ezer kenegdo* is tied directly to the story of the serpent. As Fohrman points out, there are a lot of very unusual things about this walking, talking, naked snake.[5] Somehow this snake is connected to desire and seduction. Understanding just what is entailed in "desire" will unravel the last piece of our puzzle about the role of the *'ezer kenegdo*. We can start by examining this story *backwards.* In other words, we can start by noticing some things about the resulting punishment that are not a part of our Sunday school view. By examining the end of the story, we will be able to unravel the meaning of the Tree and its relationship to Havvah.

God's curse in Genesis 3 deserves another look. Typically, we focus on the punishment God imposes. We see Adam fighting thistles and thorns in his effort to raise crops in order to survive. We feel the sweat as he works against the land, laboring in a world now turned

---

[5] David Fohrman, *The Beast that Crouches at the Door: Adam & Eve, Cain & Abel, and Beyond* (Devora Publishing, New York, 2007). Much of the ensuing discussion of desire and the Tree depend on Rabbi Forhman's analysis. I highly recommend his book.

hostile. We wince at the sound of H̲avvah in childbirth, experiencing pain in what was supposed to be fulfilled pleasure. And then we read that fateful verse, "your desire will be for your husband but he shall rule over you." We see images of the suppression of women throughout history. We think of women treated as possessions or servants. We imagine that all of this, including the supposed "biblical" justification of male domination, is contained in God's curse.

I think we have missed the point. We have certainly misread the text. It's time to look closer.

Let's re-consider exactly what is happening in this crucial story. The "curse" is not so much direct punishment as it is the beginning of difficulty, anxiety, sorrow and frustration. The judgment on humanity simply identifies frustration and pain as the inevitable consequences of an altered universe. What was supposed to be harmonious, playful, pleasant and filled with joy is *twisted*; thrown out of alignment from its original design. When sin enters the world, the entire creation is jarred loose from its proper orientation and, as a result, uninvited (but not necessarily unanticipated) consequences emerge. While there are parts of God's punishment that are genuinely prescriptive (curses), these are not assigned to Adam and his *'ezer*. God does not curse human beings. He *describes* what their world will be like now that they have partaken of the Tree. The typical theological language suggesting God "curses" human beings is mistaken. God's words to Adam and Eve are *descriptive*, not prescriptive. God describes the way the world will now be experienced. The consequences of sin are foreseen and resident in the sinful act itself. This homogenization of sin-consequence relationship is the consistent view of all Hebrew Scripture. The first act of disobedience is not out of character with every act of disobedience. Sin contains its own consequences. In the Genesis 3 account, two separate divine actions take place. One introduces new circumstances (the curses on the serpent and the land). The other elaborates realities that were implicit but are now revealed (the results for Adam and Havvah).

The difference between a *prescriptive* and a *descriptive* view of Genesis 3 is enormous and the implications for the work of redemption are radical. If the "curse" of Genesis 3 is not a new, divinely ordered punishment but rather a divine prognosis of what is now the present reality of the fallen world, then restoration is possible. Redemption is a return, a restoration of the world to its original, intended state. If the first sin brings about a divine curse that *prescribes* our destiny, then the redemptive activity of Kingdom work in this world is pointless.

Authority

Let's consider once again the original mission of Adam. Genesis 1:26 tells us the male and the female 'adam were created in the image of God and blessed by God for the express purpose of fulfilling the prime directive. Verse 27 ff. expands this original mission statement with "be fruitful and multiply, fill the earth, subdue it and rule over all living things." The summary task is to rule. Within the boundary of that task, Man is to increase, occupy (fill) and subdue.

This command has some important implications. First, God intended propagation of the human species through sexual reproduction. Man is to multiply. Sex and childbirth were commanded *before* the fall. Both were blessed. Both were to be enjoyed as the fulfillment of the command. We can rightly conclude that God's original intention for childbirth did *not* include pain. There is no point in the commonly held idea that God altered childbirth to include *extended* pain after the fall if there is no pain in childbirth before the fall. God might have prescribed pain *after* the fall (if His punishment is prescriptive), but the idea of *extended* pain presupposes that there was pain *before* the fall and God only intensifies it. This seems out of character with every description of Eden and our subsequent descriptions of the restored creation. Therefore, it appears as though something is wrong with the translation that suggests *added pain* is part of God's punishment.

Secondly, God intended Man to occupy the earth. Man's authority was to extend itself across the created world. In other words, Man was to *expand* the Garden. God originally intended Man to be the agent who brought the Garden of Eden experience to the rest of creation. The Garden was simply the model for all the rest. Adam was supposed to learn the stewardship skills in the place set apart by God in order that he could apply these skills to the rest of creation. Adam and H̲avvah are order-making image bearers. They are to extend God's order to the rest of creation. The point is clear: Man was never intended to remain in the Garden. He was designed to bring heavenly rule to the entire earth. He was to become the caretaker of the entire earth by exploring, expanding and extending God's harmony. This follows from the first part of the command. If Man is to multiply, he will require more territory. Did we imagine God intended *all* human kind to occupy the single Garden? Of course not! We were designed to take the Garden with us throughout the world.

Finally, Man was designed to subdue the earth. *Kavash* is a word of force. It is used to describe subjugating opponents, assault and military conquests (cf. 2 Chronicles 28:10, Micah 7:19 and Numbers 32:22). *Kavash* is sometimes used to describe subjugating or military force. This could be seen as the natural extension of the meaning of the word in the fallen world, a place that resists the control of Man. In its original use, *kavash* may mean simply the application of effort to accomplish the task. There is no reason to suppose Adam's life was to be one of passive indulgence. He was not designed to simply relax under a tree, picking fruit to satisfy his needs. He was designed to carry forth the project *to extend God's reign and rule.* This requires work, and work is a blessed and essential part of human existence. In fact, in this regard work is worship because it is the fulfillment of God's will. Since the implication of "multiply" and "fill" clearly involves extending the Garden, Man's assignment implies the active engagement of his skills and talents, including his God-given force. However, originally Man does not need to overcome a resistant world. Expanding the Garden around the world will take real effort and he is equipped by God to accomplish it. This is not a *man's* task. It is the task of *Man*, both male and female.

Curse

What happens to this divinely designed purpose when sin enters the world? The *method* for fulfilling God's design changes, but the *purpose* of Man does not change. Man is still created in God's image, even after the event of the first sin, and as such he is equipped and charged with the divinely designed purpose. Man is still to be God's representative of sovereignty in creation. The curse does not alter human design or purpose. It alters the *means* by which the task will be accomplished. What was intended to be a joyful exploration and expansion becomes a tedious and laborious process. *Toil* is introduced into the equation. The text reads, "you shall eat of it in sorrow all the days of your life" (Genesis 3:17). The transferred authority resident in the image of God does not disappear with the first sin. It is still there, granting both male and female their unique status. They are still God's regents, but after the introduction of sin, things are not so easy anymore.

We must give strict attention to the actual components of this curse. God *curses* the serpent. "Because you have done this, you are cursed" (Genesis 3:14). God *curses* the ground ("the ground shall be cursed because of you" – Genesis 3:17). But God does *not* curse Adam and Eve. Instead of a divine curse, the lives of Adam and Havvah will now experience "sorrow".

The Hebrew verbal root for "sorrow" is *'atsav*. Biblical synonyms include to be sad, to grieve, to become tired and weary, to become irritated, to writhe, to be bitter, to feel disgust, anguish, trouble, toil and turmoil. It's not a very nice picture. The general idea behind *'atsav* is emotional pain and distress. Imagine how the world changed when these qualities suddenly entered the picture. To get just a glimmer of the original Garden environment, all we need to do is think about life without this list of traumas. Fortunately, God's creation has not been totally erased. His glory, harmony and joy can still be found in relationships and nature. But a tragedy has befallen us. Life is now layered with *'atsav*.

In Genesis 3, God initiates *prescriptive*, judicial punishment upon the serpent. He *curses* it. God also issues a *prescriptive* judgment upon the ground, a *curse* that is the direct consequence of Adam's sin. But instead of cursing Adam and Eve, God describes the automatic consequence of their failure to obey. The consequence of their sin is not *new*. Sin did not *originate* with Adam and Eve. Although we are not privileged with an exhaustive account of the origin of sin, we know the angel Lucifer sinned in his attempt to usurp God's sovereignty *before* Havvah listened to the serpent. Sha'ul makes this quite clear in his choice of the Greek verb *eiserchomai* ("to come into, to enter") in Romans 5:12. "Even as sin *entered into* the world through one man," carries the nuance of Adam *opening the door* for sin to come into this world. Rebellion, disobedience and the consequence of separation from God already existed. Adam just let all of this disaster into this creation. God was quite familiar with the consequences of sin prior to the fall of humanity because He already experienced the rebellion of Lucifer. Therefore, God can say with absolute, existential certainty that as a result of their disobedience, Adam and Havvah will experience the natural consequence of *'atsav* as a part of human existence. He doesn't need to *command* it. He only needs to point to its inevitability.

Since the purpose of Man does not change, both male and female retain the roles of stewards, regents and priests, but these roles will now have to be accomplished in the context of *'atsav*. We can clearly see this in the description of Adam's new reality. He will still till the ground. The command of Genesis 1:28 is summarized in 2:15 in two Hebrew verbs, *'avad* and *shamar*. Literally, the two mean "to serve/work" and "to guard with great care." God places Adam in the

Garden with these two tasks before him. He is to work the Garden as servant and guardian. In this way, Adam will fulfill a part of the command of 1:28. With Havvah as his *'ezer kenegdo*, they will multiply and fill the earth and together work to subdue and rule over it. *None of this assignment changes as a consequence of the act of disobedience.* Adam's reality is still tied to the ground, but now he will experience toil. He will have sorrow, trouble, disappointment, frustration and irritation as he attempts to fulfill his divine commission. No matter how hard he works, some part of the earth will be unresponsive. He is alienated from the earth. He will be alienated from the very thing that made him, the *'adamah*. He will live with the knowledge that productive effort no longer guarantees productive results. Eventually, the cursed ground will capture him completely. He will return to the earth, an inevitable consequence of sin. He will die.

Consequence

Let's look very closely at the consequence for Havvah.

> *To the woman He said, "I will greatly multiply your pain in childbirth, in pain you will bring forth children; yet your desire will be for your husband, and he will rule over you."* (Genesis 3:16)

Does the translation suggesting increased pain in childbirth make sense? The Tanakh represents giving birth as the high point of a woman's life. It may be hard for our contemporary, planned-pregnancy generations to appreciate this perspective, but there is no question that having children was considered a blessing from God and a greatly anticipated, life-changing event in the Hebrew culture. A moment's reflection on the trauma of Sarah's barrenness gives us ample evidence of the centrality of this event. Notice that God's judgment on Havvah does not remove her role in reproduction. She is still the mother-to-be of all humanity. If the correct translation is about *birth*, then in the moment of her glory, she will discover a reminder of her disobedience. At the precise moment of fulfillment, she will experience *'atsav*.

However, I am not convinced that this verse is really about childbirth. Meyers[6] suggests this text must be about *child rearing*, not child bearing. That fits the general principle of Hebrew justice – measure for measure. Disobedience destroys relationship. The appropriate punishment is not a moment of pain but rather a life of relationship struggle. If Meyers is correct, then every parent understands why *'atsav* is in this description. Once disharmony is introduced into humanity, all relationships suffer. This certainly includes relationships with children. In fact, Meyers' suggestion offers an even deeper insight into Genesis chapter 4, the story of Cain. We will explore this in due time.

It is important to note that the Hebrew idea of justice (measure for measure) is built on the concept that the degree of sinfulness must be covered in the degree of punishment. We commonly view this as the "eye for an

---

[6] The Hebrew text could be read, "I will intensify your pain and your child bearing," not "your pain and your giving birth." The point is important. Meyers (TDOT, Vol. XI, p. 279) argues that this verse cannot be translated in the classical way about childbirth. He contends the critical word always refers to mental and emotional suffering and since neither conception nor pregnancy are sorrowful, this verse must refer to the added trauma that will accompany child *rearing*, not child bearing. It is an issue about relationships, not procreation.

eye" principle. It implies that we are not entitled to take more than we have lost as a consequence of sinful acts. The measure-for-measure principle operates in God's description of the consequences of the first sin. Adam came from the ground. The ground will now resist him. He will struggle with the very substance that was intended to be a responsive participant in his work. The same idea is applied to Havvah. She is the ultimate relationship manager. She is designed to facilitate the relationship between her man and God. Now she will discover that the "ground" of her being, Adam and the work of relationships, is laced with sorrow. This means that relationships with her children are also affected. The consequences of her sin are not limited to the single relationship with Adam. They extend to others.

In spite of the introduction of 'atsav, Havvah's divinely initiated purpose continues. She is still central to "multiply and fill" the earth. She will experience sorrow in the "ground" of her labor (relationships with husband and children) just as Adam will experience sorrow and toil in the ground of his labor. The world has become a place of 'atsav.

This correction of the Genesis 3:16 passage eliminates the traditional view of childbirth as a curse on women. But there is another factor that suggests even this correction needs enhancement. Let's consider once more the crucial passage.

To the woman He said, "I will greatly increase your sorrow and your conception – bring forth children in pain. And your desire is for your husband, and he does rule over you." Genesis 3:16 (translation SRI)

Perhaps we have become so numb to this story that we just don't ask any questions about it. We've heard about "Eve's curse" so many times that we simply assume this is what the text says. But maybe we need to ask some *very big* questions about this text, particularly in light of what this translation suggests about God.

The problem with this translation is the vowels. Hebrew has no vowels, so *any* translation will have to add vowels to the consonants in order to decide not only what the words mean but also what words are actually in the text.

There are two biblical possibilities for syllable and vowel construction in the consonants that make up the phrase translated "greatly increase."[7] Translators usually assume that the consonant construction *Resh-Bet-Hey*, a verb meaning, "to be many", is repeated, producing the translation "to be many, many," or "greatly multiply."[8] But a small shift in the pointing in the second word changes the meaning entirely. Now it is not a repetition of Resh-Bet-Hey but rather a new word, Aleph-Resh-Bet. This word, *'arab*, occurs more than thirty times in the Tanakh. It means, "to lie in wait, to ambush." If this second word is *'arab* and not a

---

[7] The consonants are Hey-Resh-Bet-Hey and Aleph-Resh-Bet-Hey. The two words look almost the same; the only difference being the initial consonant. The usual assumption is that both words come from the same stem.

[8] The Hebrew is *harba arbe* with the usual vowel pointing. The Resh in the first word is pointed with a Sheva so that it closes the syllable *Hey-Resh* in the word *Hey-Resh-Bet-Hey*. The Resh in the second word continues the same closed syllable pointing. But the pointing was added hundreds of years after the written text. If the second word is pointed without the Sheva, then Resh *begins* a new syllable and the word changes from a repetition of *rabah* to the word *'arab*.

repetition of *rabah*, then the meaning would be "has caused to increase the lying-in-wait your sorrow." Rearranged in English, God says, "The one who ambushed you has multiplied your sorrow." This makes a huge difference!

Bushnell offered this alternative nearly 100 years ago.[9] It was ignored. Why? Because for Christianity, the weight of church tradition could not imagine that God didn't curse Eve. There is nothing impossible about this translation of the Hebrew. The difficulty is that it exposes 1800 years of misogyny perpetrated by the church.

Bushnell's suggestion has further merit when we consider some other elements of this passage. Meyers points out that the proper understanding of the consequences is not about childbirth but rather about raising children. That means this text can't be about the termination of pregnancy. Viewing the text as a comment about the struggle within *relationships* is far more consistent with the fabric of the story. In a "measure for measure" world, Havvah's experience of toil is just as prolonged as Adam's. It lasts a lifetime.

This fits neatly with the consequences concerning "desire" and the husband. Personal relationships are at stake here – precisely the same issue behind the serpent's attempt to eliminate Adam. God is not issuing a curse. He is stating a fact. Disobedience will bring a mess and that mess will extend to relationship with both children and husband. She was designed as the relationship guide. Her *'atsav* will be found in the same

---

[9] Katherine Bushnell, *God's Word To Women* (God's Word to Women Publishers, Mossville, IL) 1923, p. 51.

arena. Who is responsible for all this? It's not Havvah alone. The serpent did the deceiving. Havvah listened, but the serpent spoke. Now we can see why God says, "I will put enmity between you and the serpent." What He is saying is this: I am going to make it very difficult for you to ever be deceived again by this creature. I am going to make him something other than a walking, talking, resplendent, almost human-like beast. Now he will be revolting. You will never listen to him again." In other words, from now on, any future encounters with the serpent are going to become fearful and repugnant. The walking, talking, naked snake is going to look like something horrible. You won't be listening to him anymore.

Havvah is right to blame the serpent. She is also responsible, of course, but the focus of God's observation is about the *effect* of the serpent's deception, not a prescription of dispensational punishment. If the Son is going to arrive through a woman, then the hope of Mankind rests on the submissive heart of a woman, doesn't it? Maybe this little story is about God *assisting* the 'ezer kenegdo by creating a natural revulsion between the deceiver and the woman. Maybe God is making sure that she will listen to Him, just as she is supposed to. Maybe it's all about God's heart of compassion instead of instant punishment.

On many levels, Hebrew stories are consistent in their portrayal of the character of God. Genesis presents God as honorable, orderly, loving, compassionate, forgiving and sovereign. In this passage, perhaps the most critical passage for understanding the nature of sinful human beings, do we suddenly discover a God who demonstrates wrath without the possibility of restitution? If we believe that God "curses" men and women, that's what we're saying. But if Bushnell is right, the focus of this verse is on the damage caused by the naked snake, not on the edict of a less-than compassionate Creator.

Now let's consider the second part of the statement to Havvah.

And your desire is for your husband, and he does rule over you. Genesis 3:16 (NASB)

There are two critical words here: desire and rule. The word "desire" (*teshuqah*) is found only three times in Scripture, here, Genesis 4:7 and Song of Solomon 7:10. Before we examine the second and third passages, we will have to do some research on this occurrence.

This verse has created an incredible amount of grief within the Body. For centuries the Church interpreted the verse as a prescriptive curse, claiming that God intentionally turned the tables on the egalitarianism of creation as punishment for Eve's sin. According to this interpretation, God deliberately authorized men to rule over women. In recent times, with the dawning awareness of church-based misogyny, theologians have modified this declaration claiming it applies only to husbands and wives, not all men and women. Contemporary theologians have continued to modify this basic hierarchical view.

Christians who supported male hierarchy with this verse often argued that *sexual* desire is part of the curse. Accordingly, women were forever plagued with powerful sexual desire (God saw to it) for their husbands but husbands were given the power to dominate these emotionally distressed creatures. If you find this interpretation a bit shocking, look at nearly any commentary on Genesis written between 250 AD and 1950 AD. The misogyny of the interpreters is evident, relegating women to creatures of emotional turmoil associated with a perpetual state of sexual frenzy requiring the calmer, reasoned approach of the superior male.

Of course, things have changed. Now conservative commentaries modify this interpretation by removing the sexual overtones and suggesting this is not so much a *curse* as it is a description of divine re-ordering in the post-fall world. Many theologians resist the former language of domination but they nevertheless argue that the Bible teaches wives are to be submissive to husbands as part of the way the world works in this dispensation. After all, God made it so!

Turning

In 1921, Katherine Bushnell challenged much of this interpretive scheme in her book *God's Word for Women*. According to Bushnell's research, the crucial term, *teshuqah*, has two distinct linguistic etymological backgrounds. The first follows the path of the LXX, winding its way back through ancient Syraic, Ethiopic and Arabic roots to the Hebrew text. This path provides us with the meaning "turning." With this meaning, the statement in Genesis is not about Eve's "desire." It is about Eve turning away from God and toward her husband as the center of her life. In other words, God observes that Eve's sin is the result of her decision to make Adam more important than God. She chooses to take of the fruit because she opts for *her evaluation of what is best* in the fulfillment of her role as *'ezer kenegdo*. She puts her choice ahead of God's commandment.

Bushnell was the first to point out that a major shift in translation occurred in 1528, almost 3000 years after the text was written. A Dominican monk named Pagnino translated this Hebrew word with the Latin equivalent of "lust". Bushnell demonstrates that Pagnino's translation became the basis of nearly every English translation following his 1528 publication. But the ancient translations, including the Septuagint, render the word as "turning," not "lust." This research is enormously important. With the exception of the 1380 Wycliffe translation and the 1609 Douay Bible (both translations from the Latin Vulgate), every subsequent English version adopted Pagnino's translation of "lust," modifying the term to "desire" in later works. In other words, our contemporary understanding of Havvah's relationship to Adam after the Fall is characterized by the wrong word.

God observes that Havvah's actions are described by *teshuqah* but now, in a fallen world, her husband will exercise the upper hand. The pact of mutual responsibility and harmony is broken. Now there is a battle for control. In spite of her longing to regain her previous status as the *'ezer kenegdo*, she will experience her mate's resistance. Just as the earth resists Adam, so Adam will resist his *'ezer kenegdo*. The parallel is important. The source of Adam's creation (the earth) will resist him. Where it once was the source of delight and fruitfulness, it is now the arena of *'atsav*. In parallel, the source of Havvah's creation, Adam himself, will resist her. Where it was once the arena of delight and fulfillment, it is now the place of *'atsav*. Her life will be frustrated in her attempt to fulfill both divinely commanded purposes: to bring new life into this world and to act as the protector and provider for her mate. She will have *'atsav* in field of her operations (relationships) and *'atsav* in the attempt to fulfill her intended destiny.

Now we can correct the mistaken translation of *teshuqah* as "desire". This is not about passionate wish fulfillment. What happens here is concerned with alienation from the ground of being. Adam is alienated from the earth. Havvah is alienated from Adam. This insight helps us recognize something about the second part of the declaration to Havvah. It is not possible to understand "your *turning* will be toward your husband, and he will rule over you" without recognizing there is an implied previous state where the opposite was true. The frustration of Havvah's intended role reverses what was previously a natural state of affairs. Before her disobedience, she was expected to execute her role of responsible stewardship as *avodah*, delightful work, service and worship. Now she will experience a battle doing what she was naturally equipped to do. In Genesis 3, we encounter the great collapse. Havvah still knows what she is meant to do, but now her destiny is opposed by the very one who previously recognized her perfect suitability. She seeks to be the protector and provider over the very person who now refuses to acknowledge her designed assignment. Once serving as *'ezer kenegdo* was delight and an act of worship at the same time. Now it is toil.

Adam is alienated from the very substance that provided his essential makeup. He is separated from what he is made from. This is the deepest kind of alienation. He and the earth are now at odds. His assignment doesn't change. He is still to *bless* the earth with his stewardship, but now he finds resistance. His *avodah* must be worked out in the context of *atsav*. Precisely the same is true for the women. She is alienated from the source of her substance – the man – for she came from him. She is separated from the very thing that she is made from – her husband. Her task is frustrated. She is to be his steward, to *bless* him with her care, but now he resists. She has to work out her assignment, her *avodah*, in the context of *atsav*. This is measure for measure.

Consider the psychological interactions between Adam and Havvah during and after the temptation. Notice the serpent approaches Havvah, not Adam. This is no accident. Scripture tells us the serpent was the most cunning of all beasts. What better way to defeat God's purpose than to seduce the protector and guide? If the serpent can entice her to opt for self-determination, Adam will be no problem. Furthermore, notice the serpent's appeal to Havvah lies along the same path as her destiny. She is to be the steward of Adam just as Adam is to be the steward of the earth. The serpent appeals to her desire to accomplish this task by suggesting that she will be *better equipped* to fulfill her destiny if she has the same knowledge and status as the Creator. After all, with the ability to discern good from evil *on her own*, she will rise from the role of the steward of another to the role of the benefactor of another. It is the appeal of enhancing her resident capacity that sets the sin in motion. She sins in alignment with her *strength*, not her weakness.

Adam Too

Adam's part in the temptation is also evident. He *follows* along. There is no suggestion that Adam wavered in his acceptance of Havvah's invitation. In spite of his knowledge of the direct, verbal command of the Creator, Adam accepts Havvah's decision. Of course, Adam is placed in a nearly impossible position. He must decide between Havvah and the Creator. One or the other will have to be abandoned. Given his excited endorsement of the role of Havvah in his life, is it any surprise that he participates in her choice? What we must not overlook is the fact that Adam accepts Havvah's direction, just as a child might accept the direction of an adult who is a trusted protector. Adam, of course, is no child and is equally culpable. According to the commentary in the New Testament, Havvah was deceived but Adam *deliberately* entered into the disobedience.[10] The fact that Havvah is the first one attacked and that Adam offers no resistance makes sense once we acknowledge her role as the *'ezer kenegdo*.

Adam's response to God's inquiry about his disobedience supports this understanding that the role of the *'ezer kenegdo*. Notice what Adam says: *"The woman whom You gave to be with me, she gave me of the tree and I ate"* (Genesis 3:12). Adam blames the woman. The woman blames the serpent. The serpent blames no one (it accepts the verdict). But Adam doesn't imply that the woman alone is to blame. Adam ultimately shifts the blame onto God! It isn't just the woman who is responsible for his condition. It is God Himself who created this woman to guide him. From

---

[10] 1 Timothy 2:14

Adam's perspective, the real design flaw rests with God so God is culpable for the resulting disobedience. Adam doesn't turn to the woman and say, "It's your fault!" He turns to *God* and says, "It's Your fault!"

We recognize Adam and H̲avvah are both accountable, but do we recognize how subtly Adam changes sides? Do we do the same thing when we offer an excuse to the Holy One of Israel? It's one thing to say, "Yes, Lord, I have sinned." That leads to repentance and ultimately to an acknowledgment that God's perspective on our actions is the *only* true perspective. It's quite another thing to say, "Well, Lord, I've sinned but I really couldn't help it. The people you put in my life were bad influences. You engineered my circumstances and I got overwhelmed. I mean, You're the sovereign God, so you could have prevented this if You really wanted to." We might not be so bold in our accusations, but our *actions* might be just as audacious.

Adam's excuse implies that he recognized and acknowledged the role of the *'ezer kenegdo* prior to the fall. He followed her into disobedience. He admits she was his guide. He implies that this is what he was supposed to do – to trust her decisions and act on them. That is why it is *God's* fault. Adam claims that there is a design flaw with this person whom he previously acknowledged as the ideal partner. God made a mistake, not Adam. He just did what was expected.

From "naked and unashamed" to a frantic search for covering, Adam experiences the first human betrayal. This other one, the one who is the perfect protector and guide, who is quite literally from himself, has failed in her responsibility. Adam feels as if he were betrayed by his own body. The one who stands beside him, the extension of his own being made physically visible, invites him to enter into an act of self-determination. The Genesis account is phenomenally accurate in its description of the psychological operation of sin. Sin is listening to myself, as though my own consciousness were projected apart from me in a conversation about moral choices. That is precisely what happens between Adam and Havvah. Adam joins her decision and Adam must pay the price. We can well imagine Adam's emotional reaction, deciding he will never again allow himself to simply follow this supposed *'ezer kenegdo*. From now on, he will make the decisions. As a *descriptive* statement of the consequences of disobedience, this break in the intended relationship is exactly what we see in the phrase, "your *teshuqah* will be for your husband, [but] he will rule over you."

Havvah is created as the *'ezer kenegdo*. She is seduced because she is the *'ezer kenegdo*. Adam follows her lead because she is the *'ezer kenegdo*. Her failure to uphold the responsibility entrusted to her causes Adam to reject her as *'ezer kenegdo*. Instead of forgiving, Adam assumes control, suggesting that the woman is unfit for the job. From this point forward, Adam takes the initiative. He no longer trusts his wife. Furthermore, Havvah must now *fight* to act as the *'ezer kenegdo* for her man. Sin breaks the trust relationship between Man and God and the trust relationship between male and female. The loss of innocence is not the psychological loss of unashamed sexuality. It is a loss of the fundamental ingredient for all intimate relationships – trust.

The intellectual, emotional and volitional process that led Havvah to take the forbidden fruit is exactly the same process that should have led her to embrace her role as *'ezer*. Life does not consist of two separate and incommensurable methods of operation. Life consists of two separate and incommensurable goals achieved by the *same* method of operation. That's why sin seems so easy. It uses the same design circuitry. It just chooses the wrong direction. Genesis reminds us to look at the *turning* in our behavior.

Havvah's failure calls us to see that it is possible to seek God with as much emotion, dedication and jubilation as we put into our favorite team or our most enjoyable sport or our most satisfying hobby or our greatest passion. The methodology is exactly the same. We cry over losing even the smallest contest. We feel the rush of the split-second victory. We know the "team" history like the back of our hands (it's called the Bible). We vacation at God's great places and are thrilled when He drafts a new team player. We feel the exhaustion of satisfied fulfillment or weep over agonizing defeat. We spend hours gazing over the things of God that are part of our collected memories. God could be our deepest passion.

But in all likelihood, He is not. You and I might be fanatics for football, but we are not likely to be fanatical about God. We have taken what God built into us, designed for Him, and sought out other objects of desire. Too late, we learn that the design is perfected in only one direction. We are more likely to follow Havvah in the pursuit of independent strength rather than learn to pursuit dependent obedience.

How did we get to this terrible state? For the answer to that question, we have to back up some more. We have to go back to the introduction of the serpent.

CHAPTER 8: Adam and the Serpent

Naked

Now the serpent was more crafty than any beast of the field ... Genesis 3:1 (NASB)

Adam and his wife thought they could be super-human. Instead, they just discovered they were naked. It was the greatest seduction the world has ever known. If we peek into the Hebrew in this verse, we discover a subtle wordplay that reveals just how "crafty" the serpent was.

The Hebrew word for "crafty" is *'arum*. It has positive and negative uses. In Proverbs, the word means prudent (Proverbs 14:8) or humble (Proverbs 12:23). Here it means shrewd, duplicitous or seductive. We can't see in the English translation that this is a wordplay with the Hebrew *'arom*, the word used to describe nakedness (Genesis 2:25). In fact, there are a host of consonants (A-R-Y-M) that carry nuances about this event: *'erwah* (nakedness), *'arwah* (dishonor), *'arom* (naked) and *'arum* (crafty). Do you notice something about the connections between them? The Hebrew pictograph helps: "to see a person connected to chaos." In other words, nakedness is now a symbol of *disordered* existence. There was a time when being naked was perfect alignment with the design of the Holy One. There was a time when nakedness reflected ordered, honorable relationships. Then the serpent turned nakedness against itself, using its vulnerability to bring about the destruction of the divine relationship. Suddenly nakedness became the symbol of chaos. We are the ones who behold our own chaos. We are afraid of who we are. What we lost was not innocence. It was order.

Everything important in life happens in the first three chapters of Genesis (plus an appendix). This wordplay is no exception. We discover that we are tempted to establish our order in place of God's order. We should learn that displacing God's order destroys all order – it leaves us naked and ashamed, exactly the opposite of what we hoped to achieve. We see that one time our vulnerability was the crown of humanity. We thrived in dependence on our Creator. But sin's disorder destroys our vulnerability, not by stripping away our fragile innocence but by removing the trust that makes vulnerability possible. Vulnerability without trust is chaos. That's what the serpent left us.

The biblical text reveals our predicament even in the word picture of "serpent." The pictograph of "serpent" (na<u>h</u>ash) is a fence separating life and destruction. This is precisely the role that the serpent plays. He provides a choice between life and death. He is himself the fence separating the two. What the serpent left behind is chaos incarnated, existence without belonging or connection. God's restoration appeals to our deepest loss - the loss of trust - trust between God and Man and between each other. We can cover up but we cannot hide. It takes God's provision and covering to restore our humanity.

As Adam discovered, fig leaves don't really do the job. When Adam attempted to sew fig leaves for coverings, he was trying to conceal something, but it wasn't his genitals. It was his disobedient pride. The Hebrew word pride (from the root *ga'ah*) means, "to rise up, to be lifted up or exalted." That's precisely what Adam wished to conceal from the eyes of the Lord. He wanted to put a fence around his self-exaltation, to cover his rising up against God's command. The verb *ga'ah* paints the picture, "what comes from the lifting up of strength." Adam discovered, much to his chagrin, that lifting himself up produced the necessity of privacy. Once his true identity could be openly displayed. Now it had to be concealed.

If Adam remembered *who* he was, he would not have acted as he did. The first line of defense against disobedience is a full recognition of our created status. Once Adam disobeyed God's word and denied his image-bearing existence, he discovered the terror of his idolatry in confrontation with the one true and holy God. He had to cover it up.

There is a great deal more to the serpent's seduction than a loss of innocence, just as there is a great deal more to the idea of nakedness. In order to understand how all of this affects the status of the *'ezer kenegdo* in the *fallen* world, we will have to dig deeper still. But now it's time to introduce the other player in the Garden – Adam.

Adam heard God give the command. He listened but he did not obey. As *zakar*, he was created to remember. His single obligation was to remember what God said and live accordingly. God told Adam everything he needed to know in order to maintain a perfect relationship with Him. But Adam listened to the naked snake. Adam became the first idolater. The text makes it quite clear that Adam was right there while the conversation occurred. Genesis 3:6 reads, "*she took of its fruit, and ate, and gave also to her husband with her; and he ate.*" The Hebrew translated "with her" is *'immah*. It doesn't mean he was just standing there. It means he was *agreeing* with everything as it happened. The preposition *'im* carries the meaning of something *done together or in common.* This is *not* the exclusive sin of the *'ezer*. This is mutual culpability.

We can imagine what it must have been like for Adam and his *'ezer*. They were the only human occupants of God's Garden. What joy it must have been to discover all that God put there, to walk hand-in-hand through the creative display of the Lord, observing the perfect harmony of the ordered world. Adam knew in his bones that the one walking beside him was exactly right for him, a perfect complement of physical/spiritual being. She was his trusted companion and guide. It's not surprising at all to find that he is right there during the serpent's conversation.

But it is surprising that Adam *doesn't say a word*. He doesn't object, resist or challenge anything. He submits to her suggestion and follows her lead. Why? Isn't he the one who is supposed to remember? Isn't he the *zakar*? Of course he is. When God asks him why he ate of the fruit, he offers the excuse, "I just did what she told me to do. That's what You made her for, God. She's supposed to guide me." And he's right. That is what the *'ezer* is supposed to do. She is responsible for her mate's relationship. She is supposed to guard him. Adam did what she said because he *trusted* her.

The woman fails to maintain the boundaries. She fails as *neqevah* as well as *'ezer*. She fails to recognize the difference between how she is made and how she *might be* made. As the boundary keeper, she fails to recognize her own boundaries. She steps over the line because she does not see the difference between being equipped by God and being self-sufficient. And Adam follows. He forgets that the Lord told him something else. Both the man and the woman violate their essential, God-created character. But that's what sin does. It violates who we really are. That's why sin is a form of insanity.

Was it a mistake to trust her? No. The only place in the Bible where the Hebrew word for trust (*batach*) is used positively between human beings is in Proverbs 31:11. That verse instructs a man to *trust* his wife. In every other case, the use of *batach* as a positive declaration of trust is between a man and God. Adam was not wrong to trust her. A man is supposed to trust his wife in the same way that he trusts God. Adam's problem is not trust. It's remembering. When Adam fails to be who he really is – the one who remembers – then there are no standards for trust. Remembering implies upholding God's standards. Remembering means measuring trust against truth. Trust without truth leads to sin. Trust without remembering the truth is like sailing without a compass. You can trust the wind will fill the sails and propel you forward, but you have no idea where you are going. Sha'ul was entirely correct to say, "As by one man, sin entered the world." He did not have to say, "As by one woman." Adam was right there, forgetting how God made him and what he was supposed to be. The woman was deceived but Adam wasn't. He made a deliberate choice.

We trust God because He is unwaveringly true and reliable. That is the divine standard of the 'ezer – reliability based on unwavering truthfulness. But it is not reliability based on *my* unwavering faithfulness. The 'ezer must demonstrate reliability based on God's unwavering faithfulness. In other words, she is the guardian of the borders. She is responsible to hold the boundaries in place *as God prescribed them*. Since the first sin, everyone wavers. We need an *outside* voice of correction to correspond to our inside voice of passion. We need a compass that is not influenced by *our* idea of True North. Adam forgot the truth – and his disregard killed him. Havvah ignored the boundaries – and overstepping them slew her. If you are in a complementary relationship with another, you will need both truth and boundaries before trust and direction can accomplish their purposes. Don't confuse them no matter how desirable the fruit.

Standing next to his *'ezer*, Adam participated in the rebellion. He did not vocalize a sound, but his heart shouted. His silence brought about the Fall just as much as Havvah's conversation. Adam listened and obeyed the voice of the snake instead of the voice of God. Adam is the first example of the principle that the only thing necessary for the triumph of evil is for good men to do nothing.

Unfortunately, this becomes Adam's default behavior. He becomes the manifestation of his idolatry. This isn't the only time when his silence causes generational disaster, as we shall see. But it is a critical reminder to us. Silence is not golden. Sometimes, it's godless. When we are faced with the temptation to not remember who God is, who we are and the difference between the two, we must speak up. We must listen *and obey*. We must object to any serpents that suggest our own feelings are the final arbiter of moral behavior. We must respond as the second Adam responded – "It is written."

It's All Her Fault!

Adam's excuse and his failure to accept responsibility

lead directly to his second fatal sin. Because of this second sin, Adam sets the stage for the subsequent history of male-female relationships. In fact, Adam's *second* sin becomes the precursor to the entire history of Man's interaction with YHWH. It is a tale of woe that begins with this confrontation with God.

Adam offers the following excuse: "The woman whom you gave to be with me, she gave me of the tree, and I ate." Adam attempts to shift the responsibility from himself to Havvah and from Havvah to God. "It's all her fault. Besides, You, Lord, gave her to me. What else could I do? She was designed to care for me and I was just following her direction." Do you notice Adam's excuse implies he previously understood and accepted the role of the *'ezer kenegdo* as the guide in the relationship? It makes no sense for Adam to plead that all he was doing was following her direction if he didn't accept her direction in the first place. Adam's plea implies he understands perfectly well that God gave him the *'ezer kenegdo* so that he could follow her. The fact that Adam ties his excuse directly to God's intended design means Adam knew God made the *'ezer kenegdo* as his protector, provider and guide.

Adam's statement implies his recognition of the role of the *'ezer kenegdo* as the one designed to keep him straight, it also points toward the thought that the proper exercise of her role leads directly to a state of bliss and happiness. The choice of word here underscores her role as the director of happiness. <u>She was built to bless.</u>

But something terrible has occurred. Adam proclaims the design is flawed. She was supposed to lead him to happiness. Instead, he has reaped misery, shame and humiliation. Since it was God's design in the first place, God must ultimately be responsible for this tragedy. It certainly cannot be Adam. He was only doing what was expected of him.

Adam directs his blame toward the Designer. Adam says he is in the company of the one God made to guard him, provide direction and be his guide to bliss. Adam acknowledges all this and concedes God is the one who provided it. But instead of seeing himself as the beneficiary of God's good design, Adam now *blames* God for the results. These words are the beginning of the two steps in Adam's *second* sin. The first step is the denial of responsibility. In the first step, Adam twists what God gave for good purposes. Adam shifts the perspective from the intention of God's design to the results of misuse of the design. Adam holds God responsible for *every* possibility that results from the gift God gave to him. If this sounds familiar, it should. We follow in Adam's footsteps by assigning culpability to God whenever we misuse His good creation for purposes outside of the boundaries He sets. We often experience misery as a result of that misuse and end up blaming God for the design. The lesson here is simple. God is not responsible for our failures to follow His directions. The reality of free will includes the ability to force any good gift into the service of the evil impulse. Adam's first step is to refuse to accept his own identity – the one who is called to *remember* who he is and who God is. It is the denial of his essential identity that leads to the next, tragic step.

Immediately following the description of the consequences in Genesis 3:14-19, the text reads, "And the man called his wife's name Havvah because she became the mother of all living." This seems innocuous enough, but it is not. This naming pattern is a repetition of the same process Adam exercises over the animal kingdom. In Genesis 2:19, Adam is allowed to "call" the animals according to their essential being. The same verb *qara* is used in both naming occurrences. It has the same implications, namely, authority over. The process of naming is the declaration of authority over the thing named. Adam fulfills God's descriptive warning in Genesis 3:16 regarding the woman by putting himself *above her* in an artificial hierarchy *of his own making*. By naming her, he raises himself as her authority. He demotes her to the status of an animal. It has been so ever since. Wherever the Fall dominates the relationship between men and women, men strive for authority over women. Notice that this is a result of disobedience. It is not part of the original design. It is not intended in the relationship between the *zakar* and the *'ezer kenegdo*. God does *not* name the woman. God's term, *'ezer kenegdo*, is a description of her essential purpose. It is *who* she is. But Adam now redefines her purpose. She is now relegated to the kingdom of those under his authority. This much must be clear: this hierarchy of authority is *man-made*, not part of God's design and never intended as the proper relationship between male and female. Adam is absolutely *not* establishing this artificial, post-Fall hierarchy as a fulfillment of a divine directive. It comes into play because Adam seeks *revenge*.

How can we make such a strong statement? Nahum Sarna offers an insight into Adam's naming process that reveals a much deeper animosity.

> Hebrew *ḥavvah*, which seems to be an archaic form of *ḥayyah*, could mean "living thing," life personified. This is how the Septuagint understood it when it rendered the name here *Zoe*. The vocalization suggests an intensive form, so that "propagator of life" is also a possible meaning. There might, in addition, be a word play involved, for Aramaic *hivya* means a serpent, as noted in Genesis Rabba 20:11; 22:2. In the Sifre inscription (I.A.31), the word for serpent is actually written *ḥvvh*. [11]

The implication is shocking. If Adam chose the name *ḥavvah* because of its relationship to the meaning "snake," then Adam not only asserts authority over Havvah but also gives her a name that will forever remind her of her failure and permanently associate her with the animal kingdom. In other words, Adam identifies Havvah with the animals under his authority. He *never forgives her*! He is the first to refuse forgiveness. As a result, he sets the stage for relationship animosity between the genders.

Adam's second sin, perhaps the more heinous of the two, is the direct result of his idolatry. He aligns himself with the serpent, blaming God for his troubles. He assumes the role of the Creator, assigning a hierarchy of authority that replaces God's original design. He follows the lead of the serpent in attempting to overthrow God's order. He is the one who seeks to

---

[11] Nahum Sarna, *Genesis: The JPS Torah Commentary* (The Jewish Publication Society, Philadelphia: 1989), p. 29. Kapelrud's article on *chavvah* in the Theological Dictionary of the Old Testament offers other etymological alternatives, including an analysis of the usual connection to *ḥayah* (to live). None bear the weight of this irony.

prescribe the purpose of the *'ezer kenegdo*. Now she is to serve him rather than serve God and bless him. In his actions, he exhibits the symptoms of idolatry.

There is another indication that Adam's unwillingness to forgive causes significant disruption in the divine order. It is found not in rabbinic legend but in the Genesis text itself. It comes from Havvah's perspective on the aftermath. It's time to investigate the text of Genesis 4:1.

I Don't Need You Anymore

And the man knew Havvah his wife and she conceived and bore Cain and said, "I have gotten a man (with the help of) YHWH." Genesis 4:1

Havvah will not be denied her role as *'ezer*. In spite of her husband's attempt to erase her spiritual DNA, she finds an outlet for her design. It is her son, Cain. This is a further disastrous consequence of the lack of forgiveness, as we shall see.

In his book, *The Beast That Crouches At The Door*,[12] Rabbi David Fohrman calls attention to the fact that the Hebrew language in Havvah's declaration is very unusual. In fact, it is so strange it requires a deep analysis. The analysis yields a meaning nothing like most of the English translations. Once we really understand the strange character of this statement, we will gain an insight into one of the basic conflicts affecting every human being. What the Mother of All Living really says reveals the penetrating depth of our

---

[12] David Fohrman, *The Beast that Crouches at the Door: Adam & Eve, Cain & Abel, and Beyond* (Devora Publishing, New York, 2007).

desire to be our own gods. Her attempts to recapture what she lost through sin and the resulting shattered relationship with her husband do not lead her to repentance but to manipulation and control.

It all begins with *et*. In spite of the common translation "with" in the parenthetical addition above, ninety percent of the time *et* does not mean "with." *Et* is usually an untranslatable grammatical indicator that the word following is a direct object. In most English translations of this verse, the word *et* is translated as "with," and expressed as Havvah had a child *with* God's help. Isn't that nice? It fits our Christian etiquette, bringing God into the process of conception and birth. Everything seems so theologically correct. But this is not what Havvah says.

The particle *et* is a linguistic marker indicating that the next word is the direct object of the sentence. In this case, the sacred name, YHWH, is the direct object. This in itself is remarkable. Notice that the woman is the first human being to utter the sacred name YHWH. This is God's *personal* name. Only those who know Him use His name. Havvah uses the Name, but in a very odd way. All of the context that enables us to understand what she means must be supplied or added. The text only says: "I have bought back (purchased) a man (*et*) YHWH." This is very strange indeed. The sense of the sentence indicates that the direct object of the verb *qanah* (to buy back) is not YHWH. It is *ish*, the "man" Cain. Yet the textual marker, *et*, clearly tells us that YHWH, not Cain, should be the direct object of the sentence. Therefore, the added prepositional phrase "with the help of" isn't correct. In Havvah's statement, *she acts upon YHWH in order to obtain a substitute man.* Is this even possible? Does a woman barter her children from God? Is a child the result of payment or negotiation? Of course not! Children are God's gifts. We parents receive His blessing with the birth of a child. We do not act upon (barter with) God to get a child. *We are the direct objects of His gracious benevolence.* All of the rest of Scripture endorses the idea that children are God's gift. He is the actor-subject and they are the direct objects of His action. But not for the injured, unforgiven and shamed H̲avvah.

The use of the word *et* indicates that in H̲avvah's thinking God is the direct object of her *acquisition* of a male child (notice that the translation "have gotten" also diminishes the emotional tone of the statement which is really about *bartering*). What does this imply in Hebrew? As the direct object, God receives the action of the verb from the subject. God receives the *acquiring* action from H̲avvah. H̲avvah's child is not the direct object of her acquisition. God is. Of course, this does not carry a sexual connotation. The same verse clearly indicates Adam impregnated H̲avvah. But from H̲avvah's point of view, Adam is inconsequential to the real process. H̲avvah implies that *she used God* to get what she wanted. Her words imply that she thinks of God as her genie, her special assistant, to get a special kind of child. Fohrman points out that this is H̲avvah's ultimate attempt to be like God. She enters into the *creative* process with God. She considers herself a *partner with God* in the production of new life. In fact, the language doesn't suggest that she is in *partnership* with God. It suggests that she *employs* God as her partner. Her greatest mode of creativity is fulfilled in the *acquisition* of a new man, and God is an obligated employee in that negotiation. In other words, she uses God to get what she wants and what she needs – a new object to fulfill her design as *'ezer*. She doesn't need a child. She needs a new husband.

The Torah does not make mistakes. The *et* in this verse is not accidental. Unless we pay *very close attention* to what the words actually mean, we will slip into comfortable theological clothing. But Havvah's statement won't let us. There is something really troubling about what she says. She acts as if she can manipulate God into doing her bidding. That, of course, is our problem too. How often do we say what Havvah says? Every time we pray, "Lord, help me *acquire* my plans. Help me do what I want to do." In other words, we add the *et* to our prayers when we act as though God can be enlisted in accomplishing what we want. The Mother of All Living says nothing more than all of her children. "God, give me what I want – and be quick about it."

The catastrophe of sin reaches much deeper than surface disobedience to a command about eating. Sin twists the divine relationship into a god-tool in the hands of scheming humanity. Perhaps all of Havvah's children need to step back from divine requests and ask if we have hidden an *et* in our words.

One more look at Havvah's declaration is even more frightening. Here's the crucial question: Why doesn't Havvah mention Adam in her statement? If your English translation uses the word "Adam," it is incorrect. The Hebrew reads *ha-adam*, "the man." It does not use his name. Havvah does not require a *person* to accomplish her goal. She only requires a donor. Would you and I say we got a child through God without even mentioning the spouse? Did Adam have nothing to do with all this except to provide the sperm?

There is something else going on in Havvah's announcement; something that reflects another catastrophe of the consequences of sin.

Havvah is Adam's *'ezer*. God engineered Havvah to be Adam's *'ezer* and only Adam's *'ezer*. That is the undeniable center of her existence and the final purpose of her life. That's the way God planned it. Once we truly grasp the intensity of this deliberate design, we begin to comprehend just how much human beings are bound to complementary relationship. In fact, Genesis 2:24 suggests that marriage is in some fundamental way the re-union of what was once a unity of harmonious existence. The "two shall become one" is not simply sexual. It is about recovering lost harmony.

The Need To Be Needed

Disobedience changed everything! Havvah failed in her role as *'ezer*. Adam denied his complicity and blamed her. Trust was destroyed. Harmony lost. Adam took control, refusing to acknowledge the God-designed role of the *'ezer*. Nevertheless, Adam's assertion of power did not erase Havvah's engineering. She is still *'ezer kenegdo*. The only question now is for whom? Havvah's answer: "I have *acquired* a man-child." Havvah takes back her lost identity *with her child*. It is important to notice she does not use the Hebrew word for child in her statement. She uses the Hebrew word *ish*, a word that describes a full male adult. If Adam will not let her be *'ezer*, perhaps Cain will. He has no choice in the matter for Havvah has *acquired* him.

The Hebrew verb *qanah* says it all. "To buy, to purchase, to acquire, to possess," is not the kind of description that we would expect when speaking of the birth of a child. But it could be symptomatic of revenge. "You refuse to let me be what I was made to be? I'll show you. I'll *take* what you won't give." That's the spirit of it. H̲avvah decided to make a deal with God to get what Adam refused to give her – a man who would let her be the *'ezer kenegdo* she was designed to be. We see the same results every day. The husband rejects the role of the wife as *'ezer*, so she turns that attention to her children. She will not be denied. It is who she is. But this means of fulfilling her destiny is a tragic twisting of the original design. Now her role results from a *purchase* instead of a gift. It is *teshuqah* (turning - desire) crafted to accomplish her goals. And it leads to another disaster.

Why is Adam not a part of H̲avvah's declaration? The answer is obvious. The serpent won the first round of the legendary battle. Adam is now an *obstacle* to her fulfillment. Sin brought separation and alienation, not union. Now H̲avvah decides to take matters into her own hands. She has the power to create and she uses that power to bring to life a *substitute* for her lost charge. She produces a replacement man named Cain. H̲avvah names *Kayin* (Cain), not Adam. This is another indication of her effort to regain control. Furthermore, the Paleo-Hebrew pictograph of the word *kayin* means weapon. Isn't that interesting? *Kayin* is under his mother's authority. She *names* him. She determines his essential character. He is her weapon of revenge. We will be what we are, one way or another, but one way leads to weapons for revenge, while the other way brings God's grace and forgiveness.

Cain *replaces* Adam in H̲avvah's quest to be fulfilled. Her man-child is not a gift from God. H̲avvah is determining her own destiny. Sin compounds itself. The text reveals that manipulation is at heart of the problem with broken relationships, between men and women and between human beings and God.

Now we can draw the connections to the "curse" of Genesis 3. Exactly as God predicted, Adam fulfilled his role in God's descriptive pronouncement. He took charge. He exercised dominion over his wife. In doing so, he shoved her face in her sin. Even naming her Havvah reminds her every day of her failure and her connection to the serpent. So, she went around him. She used him to get what she really needed, a new object for her built-in design. Only this time, her "man" did not come as a gift from God. He came as part of a deal. Havvah thinks she has bartered with God to get what she needs. Sin spins another layer of consequences. Her son attempts the same kind of *et YHWH* bartering later in life, and the results are also tragic. *Kayin*, Havvah's weapon, attempts to barter prosperity with the Lord by bringing *some* of his creative effort. He does not bring the best because he is in a negotiating mood. He brings what he thinks is minimally necessary to get what he wants – the blessing of YHWH. And when he is rejected, his reaction is nearly the same as his mother's – to lash out at the obstacle in his path, his brother who got the blessing.

This ancient story becomes more relevant as we uncover its rich treasure. We see the actions and issues that confront Adam and Havvah are still with us today. The world is still broken. Dominion is still an issue. What we learn from Havvah is this: when we try to manage our way *around* the consequences rather than seeking the face of the Lord and healing broken relationships, we end up worse than before. God will not be manipulated. He has provided a way of escape and that way runs directly through confession and repentance. Neither Adam nor Havvah seem to have taken that step – and life just got progressively worse. God forgives because He is compassionate. He "covers" them with the sacrifice of an animal. But that isn't the thrust of this story. Human behavior reveals the deepest issues here. *Now we see that unless we understand the whole story of the Genesis events, we will never understand why Sha'ul says what he says about men and women.*

CHAPTER 9: DNA Default

The Will to Power

We have reached the final chapter in the Genesis background behind the nature and role of men and women. This final chapter is not about the harmony of the marriage reunion as God intended it. It's not about the first sin and the resulting alienation from their assignments and each other. It's about the fallout from unforgiven lives. The end result of shattered relationships in a broken world is the reign of self-willed desire.

Rabbi Fohrman makes a point that simply cannot be ignored. In the context of Genesis 4, the word *teshuqah* is really a word about the unbelievable energy resident in every one of us to *create*. It is the deepest longing that we have – the longing to *make* something that lasts. *Teshuqah* is a part of who we are! It is very close to passion. Without it, we would cease to be human.

In Genesis 3:16, *teshuqah* is built into what it means to be a woman. *Teshuqah* is passion without divine judgment, creative desire without divine discipline. It is precisely what James calls the precursor to sin. And it is a part of every man and woman since the Fall. Havvah knew it. Now her son knows it. And we, the offspring of her *teshuqah*, know it too.

This is terrible and wonderful at the same time. When we align our deepest need to create with the gentle restraint of God, we can produce something fabulous, something that glorifies Him and blesses others. In the process, we experience who we really are and we are flooded with joy, discovering who He really is. But when we let our passionate energy serve ourselves, when we use it to *acquire* our own destiny, then something disastrous occurs. We create without God – and the result can only be unholy. God warns Cain that a force much more powerful than he can imagine threatens him. It is the passion to make himself the judge of good and evil. Once unleashed, this genie will not go back into the bottle easily.

This power to create ultimately belongs to God. We only borrow it while we live with His breath. Of course, how we use it is the really scary question, because it can also become the power to kill. You and I have this same *teshuqah*. Used in partnership with God, we create life. Used in partnership with self, we bring death. These are the only options.

The issue of authority determines the difference between being human and being an animal. There is a power and a passion residing within us. We must decide if we will use this power and passion under God's authority or under our own. If we decide to ignore God's rightful claim on our lives, then the natural hierarchy of authority granted by God is disrupted. We attempt to become our own authority. In this respect, we try to become like the gods. It is always a question of power and authority. We may domesticate the power God has given us by submitting to His rule, or we may act as though we are our own source of well-being. We can display the image of God in the dynamic actions of life – and become the human reflection of His glory – or we can attempt to create our own image – and become idolaters. One direction leads toward the full intention of being human. The other leads away from being human.

The Genesis account shows us that God designed the *'ezer kenegdo* with the purpose of blessing her mate. God established a covenant with the woman and equipped her to fulfill it. The man was the beneficiary of that covenant. The serpent attacked this design by appealing to her desire to be the best she could be. The serpent seduced the woman into believing that *adding to* God's work would improve her ability to bless her man. But everything turned upside-down. The man was alienated from the ground of his own being. So was the woman. The purpose of the *'ezer kenegdo* is not erased, but it is significantly frustrated. The man loses confidence in the guidance of the woman and refuses to allow her to be what she was meant to be. Both learn to pursue their own agendas through manipulation.

The Genesis account offers no evidence for a divinely ordained substitute hierarchy after the first sin. In fact, God's actions following the first sin reveal an attempt to restore the original design. The Hebrew combination of *labash* (to clothe) and *kotnot* (garments) appears in other important Hebrew Scriptures. The use in these other verses suggests something quite startling about God's provision for Adam and his wife; something that we would never imagine for two people who have just disobeyed God's explicit command. We find the combination of *labash* and *kotnot* in Leviticus 8:7 and 13 and Numbers 20:28. Those verses describe God's provision of the holy garments for Aaron and his sons. In other words, this phrase is used exclusively for those whom God dresses as *priests*. When God clothed Adam and his wife, He did more than cover their nakedness. He installed them both as the world's first priests. The role of Adam and Havvah as priests commissioned by God *is not erased* by the fall. In an age where there is considerable controversy concerning the role of women in the church, this insight from Genesis is incredibly important. *After* her disobedience, Havvah is still commissioned as a priestess by God Himself. God is the God who *restores*.

The rest of the Bible pursues this course of restoration. God intends to bring His children back to the Garden. This is the crucial point of the Genesis story. Once we know what God intended and why it was distorted, we can see that restoring God's order means returning to the design He put in place for the *'ezer kenegdo* and her beneficiary.

The *'ezer kenegdo* is designed to be lost in God *in order that* she may fulfill her role with her spouse. This is her special covenant commitment. She will be protector, provider, challenger and spiritual guide *in proportion to* her submission to her Creator.

A husband who prevents his wife from being lost in God, by whatever means, prevents her from being who she was designed to be. He suffers the consequences, finding himself alone at the depths of his being.

This is the legacy of the Tanakh. And now we are ready for Paul.

PART II
Hebrew Thinking in the New Testament

Chapter 10: A Hebrew New Testament

Moving Toward Paul

Most books about the role of women in the Body and the status of women in marriage begin with the controversial verses in Paul's letters. These efforts work backwards to demonstrate the connection between the statements in Paul's New Testament letters and the Old Testament Scriptures that support his claims. While these efforts are helpful, they are too often influenced by the centuries of Christian canonical understanding of the New Testament texts. Consequently, they tend to move toward the *justification* of Christian exegesis rather than first asking what the texts meant for Rabbi Sha'ul in a Hebrew context. The result is an apologetic effort to explain why Christian interpretation supports Christian doctrinal beliefs. This approach is exactly the opposite of one that begins with an analysis of the Torah foundation and then moves to see how Paul employs that foundation. Paul writes to many different groups of Messianic believers but he always employs the Torah as his source document and his authority. Therefore, we have followed the rabbinic approach – what does Torah say and how is it applied?

The first half of this book focused on understanding the Torah background. We looked in detail at the range of concepts surrounding *'ezer kenegdo*. This is the background for understanding Paul's words. Now we can move to his statements, but when we do we cannot assume that Paul treats Scripture in the same way that we do today. Paul uses what is commonly known as rabbinic exegetical techniques. These techniques are not the same as the way we handle Scriptural interpretation. Our analysis and interpretation is based on Western historical, cultural and etymological assumptions. But these are not Paul's techniques and Paul does not employ them when he writes to the congregations in Ephesus, Corinth and to his co-worker, Timothy.

Before we can make pronouncements about the meaning of the New Testament texts *for us*, we must first understand the meaning of the texts for the audience that first heard them. Put bluntly, Paul isn't Greek. He is Sha'ul, a Messianic Jewish rabbi. If we want to know what he is thinking, we will need to treat his words as they come from the thought of a Messianic Jewish rabbi.

Same Song, Second Verse

Rather than start with the New Testament verses about wives, we need to start with the New Testament's exhortations to *husbands*. If we don't understand the husband's obligation, we can't understand anything about a wife. There is no better place to find this introduction than in 1 Peter 3.

> *"Likewise, you husbands, dwelling together with your wives according to knowledge,"* 1 Peter 3:7

It is unfortunate that Christianity has been slandered with the idea that wives are to be the submissive slaves of their husbands. Only sloppy exegesis could have distorted the concept of submission in this way. Any careful scholarly treatment of the New Testament texts will show that submission (*hupotasso* in Greek) is a concept central to every Christian's life because it was central to the life of Yeshua Himself and is an essential element of Torah obedience. Submission is not gender sensitive nor is it restricted to marital status. It is the mark, indeed the obligation, of every believer. Without it, Christian living is a farce.

Statements in Peter's first letter contain potent strategies designed to assist both husbands and wives in the only goal of marriage that matters – becoming one. In order to accomplish this task, we must carefully regard the obligations placed on *husbands* before we attempt to understand the strategy offered to wives. Peter establishes those obligations in one short verse. But the implications are deep and demanding.

Peter begins his exhortation to husbands with an important but often overlooked conjunctive. "Likewise" is the Greek word *homoios*. Notice that this same word is used to introduce the discussion of the behavior of wives, a discussion that clearly involves the concept of submission. In that previous discussion, the word *homoios* connects us to the thoughts of Chapter 2. *Homoios* acts as a relational bridge. It literally says "in the same way". In what same way? To answer this question, we must look back at the material in Chapter 2. We discover that Chapter 2 is concerned with the purpose of suffering as participation in the same pattern demonstrated by our Lord. In other words, Peter is echoing Jesus' very words, "If they persecuted the Master, will they not also persecute the followers?" Peter is telling all Christians that fellowship with Jesus is a fellowship of suffering and that we are to engage in this suffering in the same way that Jesus did. We are to submit our lives into the hands of the Father, just as Jesus did, without reprisals, without threats and without complaint because there is a greater purpose here. For Christ, that purpose was the redemption of men who were enemies of God. It is exactly the same for us. The purpose of submission for Christian wives is the redemption of their disobedient husbands. Isn't this part of the role of the *'ezer kenegdo*?

Now Peter draws on this context. He introduces the topic of the obligation, purpose and goal of being a husband with a word that refers the reader back to the discussion in Chapter 2. "Likewise", he says to husbands. In just the same way, and for the same reasons, *husbands* are called to submission. It is the voluntary act of putting themselves under authority for a purpose. This submission has the same theological base as the submission of wives – God is in charge. God's sovereignty is the final authority in the universe. Jesus demonstrated the proper attitude of submission under the Father and husbands are called to follow His example.

"Likewise" establishes the purpose. "Dwelling together" establishes the goal. The verb "dwelling together" is *sunoikein*. The LXX translated the Hebrew *yada* with this Greek verb in reference to sexual intercourse within marriage. This is a fully active marriage relationship. There is no doubt we are within the context of "one flesh". Of course, the Hebrew background of *yada* is much richer than sexual relations alone, as we discovered in our analysis of the Genesis story. In this context, certain requirements are placed on the husband. Notice that there is no mention of the wife being a believer. While the discussion in 1 Peter 3:1-6 targets wives with unbelieving husbands, this verse does not discriminate. A Christian husband is to act this way regardless of his wife's spiritual condition.

Peter adds something of incredible value to this exhortation to husbands. He says "according to knowledge". There are several words for knowledge in Greek. Understanding the differences between them is critical. One is *ginosko*. It is a word that means knowledge that comes from external evidence and experience. This is knowledge that we gather from living, observing and testing. This knowledge comes through the process of education. By contrast, the Greek word *oida* has a different implication about knowing. This is knowledge that comes intuitively. It is not pieced together slowly by gathering information. It comes complete. It is a fully formed insight, a personal revelation.

Here Peter uses a form of *ginosko*. Peter emphasizes present but fragmentary knowledge gathered from experience in contrast with clear and exact knowledge. Peter connects the idea of "dwelling together" and "knowledge" with the Greek word *kata*. This word tells us that there is a relationship between the two thoughts. Our dwelling together must be regulated by a certain kind of knowledge. The sense of this phrase is "living together in marital harmony according to the best understanding you have at the present". Notice that it is the obligation of the *husband* to be as informed as possible – to have as much of this kind of knowledge as he can about things that matter in marital co-habitation. But we're not quite finished. Peter has hidden some treasure here.

Peter is a Hebrew writing in Greek. In order to understand his thoughts, we need to look at the Old Testament, not the Greek culture. It is clear that this letter was written to Messianic believers. They were also thinking in Hebrew thought forms. When Peter tells the husbands reading his letter that they must "dwell" (Hebrew: *yada*), every Jewish man knew exactly what he was saying. This is about contentment and peace in the marriage bed. Now Peter says, "*kata gnosin*". The same root word that would have been translated with the Hebrew *yada* is present here. Peter is literally saying "*yada* according to *yada*".

How would a Hebrew husband hear this phrase? The key is in the multifaceted word *yada*.

Yada places Peter's exhortation within the context of the Hebrew understanding of marriage. That context is permeated with the symbols of the covenant relationship. If *yada* drives us back to the first couple, it also drives us back to the first marriage – a marriage instituted by God.

No Hebrew husband could have missed this allusion. The use of "dwelling with" in Greek employs a sexual connotation that could only be expressed in the Hebrew thought *yada*. And *yada* would immediately remind the listener of the first sexual encounter ("and Adam knew Eve his wife") and the context of that encounter. It would drive the husband deep into his own heritage and the knowledge he had of the original marriage referenced in Genesis 2:24.

Husbands who read Peter's words would immediately remember the Hebrew terms for "forsake" and "cling." Both words deal with the concept of loyalty. The implications are obvious. God establishes the marriage covenant as a living human witness to the actions He requires in His covenant. We are to "forsake" the old family loyalties – our ties to this world – and "cling" to the newly created union. Properly understood, marriage is God's sacramental symbol of His covenant. This is "*yada* according to *yada*". It is covenant, sacred, holy and symbolic. Clearly, the husband's obligation in covenant relationship with his wife carries a very heavy spiritual weight.

Of course, in a Christian household, the first order of business is the spiritual condition of the marriage and that entails the full submission of the husband to his Lord and Savior. The covenant relationship that he enjoys with his Lord is to be transferred *in like manner* to the covenant relationship with his wife. This requires complete loyalty, fidelity and exclusivity. Without this first step, all the rest of the knowledge he gathers is wasted.

With this background in mind, we can look at the actions that a Torah-observant husband must take. First, he must recognize that his wife requires consideration for no other reason than she is a woman. Of course, with our study of the idea of the *'ezer kenegdo*, we now know that this consideration has very little to do with physical or gender differences. She is not to be treated as a man. She is to be treated as God's covenant blessing design for the husband. She is to be recognized according to the *purpose* God designed for her. She is special.

Peter's word choice to describe this recognition of unique status strikes us as chauvinistic today. The phrase is "as with a weaker vessel." It is unfortunate that we often read this verse with machismo. "Hey, I'm a man. I'm stronger, tougher, bigger. She's a *weak* woman. No wonder I should be in charge." But is that what Peter says? Does he really suggest, contrary to everything he knows about submission and about God's original design, that the reason men should be in control is because they are stronger? Perhaps we need to take a closer look at Peter's choice of words.

The Greek is *asthenestero*, a word that means "without strength". However, in the LXX this word translates many different Hebrew words, for example Genesis 29:17 where the context means gentle or tender, Numbers 13:18 and Job 4:3 where it means feeble, 2 Samuel 13:4 where it means puny, 2 Samuel 13:4 where it means the oppressed poor, or Psalm 6:3 where it means faint with despair. We could go on since there are many more examples, but I think you can see the problem. This Greek word has *no* uniform one-to-one correspondence with Hebrew. It all depends on the context. That means that we can't really determine what Peter had in mind from a Hebrew perspective. We have only the Greek – "without strength". And that leaves us with this conclusion. So what? There is simply too much flexibility in the Hebrew to allow us to conclude that Peter is saying anything more than what is *generally* physically true. There is absolutely no way to conclude from Peter's use of *asthenestero* that men are superior to women. In fact, to draw the conclusion that Peter prescribes a divine hierarchy of male superiority from this verse is to ignore everything we have learned about the Torah's description of Woman. We can only read this phrase as a statement of male superiority if we wrench it free from the *'ezer kenegdo* of Genesis; something Peter would most certainly never do.

However, if we reflect just a bit more on the idea of weakness in Scripture, we can see something deeper here. God is the God of **weakness**. John Timmer says, "God's power is at work in our weakness and our dying rather than in our strength and our living." We all know this is true, and we are all grateful that it is true. Without it, the foundations of our relationship to the Father would be shaken beyond repair. Peter knew this better than anyone. Peter, the strong, brash, overly confident disciple had to learn the power of weakness before he could be useful to the Lord. Don't you suppose that a man who had to discover weakness in a most dramatic way would hold up weakness as a divine *prize*?

Peter is *not* endorsing physical prowess as a rational for authority. In fact, this is a man who knew that God's strength is displayed in human weakness. The "weaker" vessel she might be, but that brings her more in line with the way God uses human beings. That is something every "stronger" vessel must honor and it is in perfect alignment with the deeper spirituality of the *'ezer kenegdo*.

Peter might have written, "Husbands, you may be stronger, but be careful that your strength does not lead you to diminish the God of weakness who put you in community with the one who represents the power of weakness. Do not sin in your strength. Learn humility in the presence of "the weaker vessel." If you don't, do you think the God of weakness will be able to use you?"

Peter continues. Husbands are to grant their wives honor. Peter's choice of the word for "grant" is *aponemontes*. It means "to assign, to bestow or to give". All of these terms are expression of *recognition of position*. You cannot *grant* honor to someone whom you do not hold in the highest regard. In addition, the biblical idea of granting honor has an interesting twist (doesn't it always?). What does it mean, biblically, to *grant* honor? We should notice that granting always begins with God. I cannot grant to you what God has not first given to me, because God is the owner of all and the final authority. Therefore, giving honor to my wife begins with God's perspective on the matter, namely that she is the *'ezer kenegdo*. Granting honor is a reflection of God's authority and it must be done in accordance with God's priorities. Our previous exploration of *radah* and *mashal* demonstrate that granting honor is inherently the task of a *representative*, not the task of the final authority.

Secondly, granting honor is an expression of recognized exaltation. We aren't left in the dark on this one. The word for "honor" is *timen*. Peter uses this word when he describes the final revelation of our faith at the return of Christ. Obviously, this is a word of some importance. We do not grant honor or assign honor to those whom we consider inferior. Clearly, Peter has no notion of superior and inferior ranking. The two words together indicate recognition of proper position – a position that is worthy of high respect. The husband is to *deliberately* give honor to his wife. The full range of meanings for *timen* includes respect, value, dignity and worth. This word connects us directly to the etymological discussion of *neqevah*. Furthermore, the Old Testament image of honoring God must have been on the minds of his readers. The Hebrew word picture of *kaved* is the open hand offered into the door or pathway. You can imagine someone extending a welcoming hand to you while ushering you into his home. *Honoring is an invitation to enter.* When we honor God, we extend an invitation for Him to come into our lives. When we honor our wives, we invite them in to who we are.

Let that sink in a bit. You don't honor your wife by putting her on the pedestal, buying her diamond rings or sending her flowers *unless* those acts are accompanied with an invitation for her to enter into your life. To honor her is to recognize her place in *your* world – a place where you let her into every aspect of who you are. In fact, you *dishonor* her when you endorse or maintain any agenda, status or hierarchy that does not promote the two of you becoming *a single entity* – one flesh – before your Maker. Peter knew exactly what he was talking about. It wasn't about separating husband and wife in some artificial relationship of superior and inferior. Honor erases all that! Honor is an open door policy. Peter asks, "Do you, husbands, honor your wives? Have you really let them in?"

The importance of honor can be seen in the next thought, "as a fellow-heir of the grace of life". "Fellow heir" is really "co-heir" (*sugkleronomoi*). This word comes from two Greek words that mean "allotments together". It is stronger than the translation "fellow-heir". It suggests *one* allotment shared by both parties. It is not an equal lot but the same lot. Here is a word that perfectly pictures God's plan for marriage – one flesh sharing in one purpose. In this case, the husband is to ensure his partner is sharing the same allotment in "the grace of life" – *charitos zoes. Charitos* is from *charis*, the word for grace, rejoice, joy, pleasure, gratification, acceptance, kindness, benefit, thanks and gratitude. We can see how all encompassing this expression is. Marriage is a single allotment of grace, rejoicing, joy, pleasure, gratification, acceptance, kindness, benefit, thanks and gratitude. The *husband is responsible* to ensure that all of these attributes of *charitos* occur in his marriage. This is the result of *"yada* according to *yada"*. These are covenant attributes.

Peter is reaching the end of his commentary on Torah obligations for marriage. There is only one more part of the verse – the consequences for ignoring these instructions. We should notice that even though Christian circles have often placed emphasis on Peter's instructions to wives (verses 1-6), the responsibility of husbands cannot be dismissed. In fact, if you go back to those first six verses, you will find that they are filled with *practical* advice for dealing with husbands who are not fulfilling their God-given assignment. The instructions to wives are not spelled out in *covenant* language. You don't find words like "honor," "co-heir" or "grace of life" in that section. You find these Scriptural covenant terms here – applied to the responsibility of husbands. Maybe we need to see this shift in emphasis *before* we go running off proclaiming that the husband is the "head" of the home. Maybe the husband *qualifies* for leadership in the home only insofar as he is fulfilling his covenant-language responsibility. And if that is the case, then there is nothing as important as *equal* inheritance. Don't spiritualize this one. You could read this as if it is about sharing in love and legacy or calling and comfort, but co-heirs is probably most often observed in handling the assets of marriage. A man who withholds the purse strings probably also withholds grace.

Certainly "grace of life" includes far more than what is in the bank account. Peter is interested in the full meaning of grace, just as God is interested in grace as the basis for our inheritance with Him. But grace is evidenced in very practical ways. One of those is money management. There's a reason why Jesus talked more about money than almost any other subject. Too often our use of money is an indicator of our real life values. In marriage, that indicator demonstrates our real application of "co-heirs in grace." What's the most important thing in your wallet - the paper with some dead man's face on it, or the picture of the one who shares your life?

Peter concludes this verse with a thought that should cause every Christian man to sit up. He says that just as there is a purpose ("likewise"), there is also a goal. In both cases, the goal is intensely personal. For wives, it is the redemption of their unbelieving husbands. For husbands, it is "so that your prayers may not be hindered."

The goal of bestowing honor and acting according to knowledge within the marriage is unhindered prayer (*ekkoptesthai* - literally, "cut off"). The picture here is cutting a branch from a tree. This is a clear reminder of Jesus' analogy of the vine and the branches. The result of "cutting off" is to render the branch incapable of producing fruit. The phrase actually says, "that your offering of prayers may not be cut off". What an amazing claim! Peter is saying that marital harmony, the responsibility of the husband, has a direct affect on the effectiveness of prayer. There is a saying, "Happy wife, happy life". But according to Peter, more than life in this world is at stake. "An honored wife yields a spiritually effective life".

Peter is giving us an indisputable spiritual law of life. If you're not fulfilling your responsibilities toward your wife, you are going to have lead-balloon prayers. You don't have to go to the marriage counselor for this one. Just ask yourself, "How's my prayer life?" "Am I feeling

God's vibrancy? Do I see victories? Is my heart being molded into His character? Am I able to clearly and confidently approach His throne?" You know the answers without having to take a course in spiritual awareness. Peter gives you the straight scoop on this – man to man. If you have neglected mutual submission, if you don't do all you can to understand her, if you haven't seen the power in her weakness, if you withhold equality in inheritance, if you're not delivering grace of life, if you don't recognize her as *your blessing*, then *you* are going to have a hard time with God. Don't give me the excuse that you are the head of the home. Forget that! If you aren't treating your wife according to these Torah-commentary principles, the only home you are the head of is the doghouse.

Peter boils it down to a short and sweet sentence. How's your prayer life? No getting around it. As a Christian man, *you are responsible*! That's what it means to be a leader in the home. It's not about *authority*. It's about *responsibility*. You are the first on the list of responsible persons. You have the divinely ordained privilege of being the one God will examine *first*. How does it feel to be the *head* now?

Peter's background highlights the crucial role played by the husband in the covenantal symbolism of marriage. It should not be surprising, given what we know about the *zakar*, that the male is responsible for the correct application of God's instruction. He is to *remember* and *obey*. Peter teaches that the husband is to remember to:

1. Demonstrate *submission* as the first principle of relationship, as a model of Yeshua's submission to the Father.

2. Exercise every capacity and take every opportunity to truly know his wife, with the same intensity he exhibits in knowing God.

3. Live in marital harmony in a way that expresses the full range of *yada*.

4. Recognize that she is a woman in the full sense of God's design and *take responsibility* to insure this is no inhibition to the purposes of the union or the fulfillment of her design.

5. Show her honor by deliberately bestowing on her the place she deserves as *'ezer kenegdo*, the one God assigned as protector, boundary-keeper and guide.

6. Honor her as a priestess designated by God, a full member of His Kingdom and a child chosen by Him to represent Him in marriage and in the world.

7. Treat her with exact equality in the inheritance of grace, operating on the fact that there is *one* share held by both.

8. Remember that efficacy in prayer is a *direct* function of personal faithfulness, loyalty and fidelity in this "glued together" relationship.

Peter's insights set the stage for our look at Paul. The keys to Paul are the same: the meaning of submission, faithfulness, knowledge and honor. Just as we cannot dislodge Peter from his Hebrew background, so we cannot ignore the Hebrew thinking behind Paul. Paul's exegesis may be more technically developed and more intricate, but the bigger picture is the same. Neither man can be understood outside of the Torah community.

CHAPTER 11: Rabbi Sha'ul

Paul and the Tanakh

The next step in our journey is pretty simple. We have established that the Tanakh teaches the equality of men and women, the mutual assignment of the task of acting as regents of the Lord and the special role God designed for the *'ezer kenegdo*. Now we need to show that Sha'ul (Paul) was a Torah-observant rabbinic scholar who never taught anything that contradicted the Tanakh. If we can show this to be a reasonable conclusion from the evidence, then it follows that Sha'ul's comments about women in his letters *must be interpreted in light of rabbinic commitment to the Torah*. In order to demonstrate this second crucial step, we will have to substantiate two related claims. The first is this: first century rabbinic Judaism generally did *not* exclude women from full participation in the synagogue or other facets of community life. We will find some rabbinic comments to the contrary. After all, rabbis were notorious for dissenting opinions. What we need to show is substantial evidence that an important group of rabbis accepted women as equals in the spiritual community. Once we have established the existence of this rabbinic position, we will then show that Sha'ul aligns himself with this group. This will provide us the grounds necessary to question the common interpretation of the difficult texts and suggest solutions that are consistent with Sha'ul's understanding of Scripture and his theological roots.

Fortunately, a lot of this work has already been done. Rather than regurgitate the contributions of scholars, I will simply summarize their findings and refer to their books and manuscripts. Perhaps the first of these men is Brad Young, Professor of Biblical Studies at the Graduate School of Theology at Oral Roberts University. His contributions in *Meet The Rabbis: Rabbinic Thought and the Teachings of Jesus*[13], *Jesus the Jewish Theologian*[14], and *Paul the Jewish Theologian*[15] provide significant evidence that Jesus and Paul were both part of the rabbinic Pharisaic teaching movement. Many recognized scholars are beginning to question the standard church model of Paul. Among those offering significant evidence that Paul was not a "convert" to Christianity and that he remained a devout, Torah-observant, Jewish, rabbinic Messianic believer are John Gager[16], Robert Gorelik[17] and Pamela Eisenbaum.[18] In addition, works by Craig Keener[19] and Gilbert Bilezikian[20] offer worthy reconsideration of the usual interpretation of Paul's writings on the subject of women.

Let's see what happens when we read the controversial passages about women and wives from a Jewish perspective.

---

[13] Brad Young, *Meet The Rabbis: Rabbinic Thought and the Teachings of Jesus* (Hendrickson: Peabody, MA, 2007).
[14] Brad Young, *Jesus the Jewish Theologian* (Hendrickson: Peabody, MA, 1995).
[15] Brad Young, *Paul the Jewish Theologian* (Hendrickson: Peabody, MA, 1997).
[16] John G. Gager, *Reinventing Paul* (Oxford University Press, 2000).
[17] Robert Gorelik has a large body of material available at www.eshavbooks.org
[18] Pamela Eisenbaum, *Paul Was Not A Christian: The Original Message of a Misunderstood Apostle* (HarperOne, New York, 2009).
[19] Craig S. Keener, *Paul, Women and Wives: Marriage and Women's Ministry in the Letter of Paul* (Hendrickson, 1992).
[20] Gilbert Bilezikian, *Beyond Sex Roles: What the Bible Says about a Woman's Place in Church and Family* (Baker Books, 1985).

The controversial passages include (by category):

Women in the community

1 Timothy 2:11-15	Women and teaching
1 Timothy 3:1-13	Women and roles within the Body
1 Corinthians 11:2-16	Women in worship
1 Corinthians 14:31-40	Women and silence
2 Corinthians 11:3	Women and deception
Romans 16:7	Women apostles
Romans 16:3-5	Women leaders
Romans 16:1-2	Women administrators
Acts 21:9-10	Women prophets

Women and marriage

Ephesians 5:21-33	Submission and headship
1 Corinthians 7: 1-5	Sexual relations in marriage
1 Corinthians 7:10-16	Marriage and non-believers
1 Corinthians 7:7-9	Remaining single

CHAPTER 12: Women in the Community

Silence

Let a woman learn in silence, in all subjection. But I do not allow a woman to teach, nor to exercise authority over a man, but to be in silence. 1 Timothy 2:11-12

When we approach one of Paul's most controversial verses, we need to fill in a lot of context before we start making universal pronouncements. The context is what is happening to Timothy in Ephesus. This is a *personal* letter of advice and counsel. It addresses issues in Timothy's ministry. It is not like the general letters Paul wrote to congregations. In this letter, Paul tries to help Timothy deal with disruptions in his ministry. If we are going to understand what Paul says and why he says it, we must first understand what is happening in Timothy's circumstances. From everything that we can gather (since we only have half of the conversation), we discover that Timothy was dealing with several heretical teachings.

First, Paul tells Timothy to combat those who propose "myths and endless genealogies" as a way of spiritual enlightenment. He instructs Timothy to stick with the pure gospel. We should notice that in this emphasis Paul states, "The Law is good."[21] In fact, Paul's primary concern is orderliness, in life and in worship. Therefore, he emphasizes the structure that the law provides. He advises Timothy to stick with the basics. Remain faithful to God's revealed instructions. Don't get carried away in speculations. Paul tells Timothy to remember the teaching of Torah that has been part of

---

[21] 1 Timothy 1:8

his education since he was a child. This comment can only be applied to the Tanakh.

Next, Paul recounts his own woeful past, emphasizing that the gospel of grace that saved him is completely adequate as a means of salvation for all who adopt it. The Messiah Yeshua brings grace beyond measure, just as God's Word proclaims. The mark of a believer is faith and good conscience. Those who depart from this foundation are shipwrecked. Paul has addressed the theological heresies. He points to grace, the Word and the heart. Without these, nothing else matters.

Now Paul turns his attention to practical matters. The first is prayer. Pray for everyone, he says to Timothy. Why? Because God desires all to be redeemed through the *one and only* mediator, Yeshua. How is this to be done? In proper order, with circumspect behavior, showing honor to God. This becomes the basis for Paul's commentary on activities in the church. He exhorts men to pray earnestly everywhere they have opportunity. He exhorts women to do the same, dressing in appropriate attire. What does he mean? He means that neither men nor women should call attention to themselves but rather act and dress in such a way that honor God. Notice the word, "likewise" in verse 9. Paul wants men to pray without anger or doubt. Then he says he wants women to do "likewise." The Greek word means "in the same manner." The only similarity here is the demonstration of attitude in prayer. This implies that women are to *pray with a similar outward demonstration*, adorning themselves to fit that attitude. Unlike contemporary Christian prayer, almost all prayer in Jewish circles was vocalized and public. People simply did not pray silently to themselves. Like the other parts of community worship, prayer was audible. Since Paul is drawing an analogy between the attitude of men in prayer and the attitude of women in prayer, this implies that the women are *speaking* prayers just as the men are. Paul's emphasis is not on what they wear. Paul emphasizes the image they bring to the spotlight. Men must be careful not to let anger or doubt take center stage. Women must be careful not to let pride and appearance take center stage. But *both* men and women are called to *speak* prayers in the worship service.

Then Paul addresses the next problem of orderliness in the congregation. This time Paul uses the *singular* Greek word *gune* (a woman), not the plural *gunaikas* (women). This leaves us with two possible interpretations. In English, this could mean a singular class noun, that is, a reference to all people in the class "woman." But it could also mean a particular woman. In other words, Paul may be saying, "Let this woman," a particular woman whose name is withheld, not be allowed to teach. Since Timothy would know exactly whom Paul meant, Paul does not need to spell it out. A woman in the congregation was teaching heretical views. She is to be forbidden to do so. It is significant that Paul shifts from the plural in verse 9 to the singular in verse 11. If he wanted to speak about *all* women, why wouldn't he simply continue to say "Women must learn in silence," or "Women are not permitted to teach"? The claim that the text teaches that all women excluded from teaching men is not the only possible interpretation. In fact, excluding women from teaching stands in opposition to the instructions and narrative of the Tanakh. Therefore, we are entitled to claim that

Paul's remarks are most likely directed at one particular woman.

Priority

Paul's first letter to Timothy continues:

For it was Adam who was first created, and then Eve. And it was not Adam who was deceived, but the woman being quite deceived, fell into transgression. But she shall be preserved through the bearing of children if *the women* continue in faith and love and sanctity with self-restraint.[22]

Notice the italicized words in this translation. In the last verse, the *addition* of "the women" shifts the meaning of the statement from a single woman to women in general. But this addition is strictly the interpretation of the translators. It has *no basis* at all in the Greek text itself. The translators *assume* that the first occurrence of "the woman" is a singular *class* noun, not a noun about a particular woman. Consequently, they add a plural noun (the women) to the second sentence. But if Paul is speaking about one particular woman, then the comment he makes about preservation in childbirth also applies to this one particular woman.

Once we recognize the imported theology in the translation, we are no longer required to interpret this text as if it applies to all women. If Paul is speaking about one particular person in Timothy's congregation, his remarks no longer constitute a general ruling. Just as Havvah was deceived, so this woman is deceived.

---

[22] 1 Timothy 2:13-15 NASB

Paul sees similar patterns in these two cases. He hints at another childbirth, connecting that birth with the possibility of salvation. The Greek text does *not* say, "childbearing," but rather "*the* childbearing," using the definite article. This indicates a particular, unique childbearing event.

> 'The childbearing" refers to the one mediator between God and persons, the person (Messiah Yeshua) (1Tim 2:5), the promised seed of Eve, the Child born of a woman (Gal 4:4). The issue at stake here is salvation, not motherhood. Women aren't saved by getting pregnant and having babies. They're saved by the child who was born—(Yeshua)! Throughout this passage, Paul was talking about how men and women are redeemed (2Tim 2:1-7), not about how they procreate. The central truth of this entire passage is (Yeshua) and God's desire for all to be saved through the promised childbearing.[23]

Gorelik points out that "the word *salvation* can mean several different things. It is possible that Paul had this woman's *restoration* in mind. Perhaps he was expressing the hope that she would realize "the error of (her) way," repent of her over-bearing nature and be reconciled to the community."[24]

Deception

What do we do about Paul's apparent disparaging remarks about Havvah's deception? Actually, what Paul

---

[23] Loren Cunningham, *Why Not Women: A Biblical Study of Women in Missions, Ministry and Leadership* (YWAM Publishers, 2000), p. 224.
[24] Gorelik, p. 88.

says is absolutely true. Adam was created first, but as we now know from our study of Genesis, this provides no grounds for a hierarchy of authority. Adam was not deceived. Havvah was deceived. But once again, Genesis tells us that although deception was not cast at Adam's feet, he did not escape culpability. His sin was not remembering and being obedient to the command of the Lord, accusing God of malfeasance and refusing to forgive. Adam might not have been deceived, but this certainly does not exonerate him! We know that Havvah sinned in her strength. She was deceived into believing that she could fulfill her role as the *'ezer kenegdo* with greater alacrity if she extended her potential. She failed to maintain the boundaries set by God and to be content with His design for her. But is her sin so unimaginable? Is it so monstrous? She is deceived. Her sin is the result of passion – the passion to be more of what she was intended to be – a sin that seems to be quite common to human beings. Recognizing that she was deceived, by the way, implies that her sin was not a transgression based on evil motives. It is a sin nevertheless, but one wonders if it doesn't fall under the category of unintentional sins rather than deliberate and willful transgressions. The resulting disaster certainly is unanticipated.

It's worth noting that Paul uses two different but related verbs when he describes Adam's behavior and Havvah's transgression. Adam was not *epatethe* (deceived) but the woman was *exapatetheisa* (deluded). What is the difference? The first verb (*apatao*) means "to be led astray or seduced into error." Paul writes that Adam was not led astray or seduced. The implication is that Adam willingly participated with full knowledge of his decision. The second verb means "to be completely duped, to deceive completely." Paul writes that Havvah was completely deluded. Examine the implications here. To say that Adam was *not* deceived can only mean that Adam disobeyed knowingly. He violated the command given to him with full knowledge of his disobedience. He was *not* deceived. Havvah, on the other hand, transgressed the command in a state of deception. She somehow thought that she was *not* transgressing the will of God in her action. She was wrong in that evaluation, but according to the interpretation of Paul, she did not sin with malice aforethought.

Now that we see the difference in these verbs, do you still imagine that Paul exonerates Adam because he was *not* deceived? Perhaps Paul's declaration to Timothy emphasizes how much more Adam is culpable. In this context, Paul does not emphasize Adam's superior moral position. Paul emphasizes the fact that Havvah was capable of being completely duped by the enemy. In like manner, the woman in Timothy's congregation is also being completely deceived by false teaching. Her intentions may be good. She may not be motivated by malice or anger or spite, but the result is no different than the consequences to Havvah. She is outside the will of God.

None of this allows any moral high ground to Adam or to men in general. As far as Paul's letter to Timothy is concerned, all we can conclude is that this woman has repeated the pattern of Havvah's error. Paul sees it, warns Timothy about it and offers a statement of hope for her restoration, all of which is consistent with the Torah.

One Woman Among Many

Notice the last element of Paul's instruction to Timothy concerning the woman. *"But I do not allow a woman to teach, nor to exercise authority over a man, but to be in silence."* Bilezikian convincingly argues that:[25]

1. the meaning of the text here is under considerable debate, particularly because Paul's choice of the Greek word translated "authority" is never found anywhere else in the New Testament and is not the usual word for authority.

2. on the surface, the text seems to violate an established core value of the redeemed community; namely, the removal of distinctions common in the world (Jew-Gentile, male-female, slave-free). Paul himself endorses the rejection of these distinctions so it seems patently unlikely that he would contradict himself here.

3. interpreting the passage as a restriction for women in the believing community contradicts Paul's explicit teaching about the use of spiritual gifts by both genders, the uniform commitment to teaching the word by *all* believers, the active participation of women in ministry (with his full endorsement) and the weight of the evidence in the Tanakh.

The admonition to silence is consistent with the rabbinic practice of repentant meditation when one is confronted and determined to be out of alignment with the truth. Followers of God are to learn the truth in

---

[25] see Bilezikian, *Beyond Sex Roles*, pp. 174-178.

submission to the one who instructs them in God's way. Then they are ready to complete the purpose of learning, that is, to teach others. Paul's admonition is not about *all* women. It is about this particular woman, who has been deceived. She is to enter into a time of silent meditation under the tutelage of competent instructors in order that she may find the error of her ways and be rescued from her difficulty. Interpreting the passage this way is consistent with rabbinic practice and with Paul's own approach to similar problems among communities. Furthermore, it follows the spirit of the teaching on the role of women in the Tanakh.

As The Law Says

Before we look at Paul's remarks to Timothy concerning leadership roles for women, we can take a quick glance at the other passage where Paul seems to suggest women should be silent in worship. That passage is the notorious verse in 1 Corinthians 14.

Let the women keep silent in the churches; for they are not permitted to speak, but let them subject themselves, just as the Law also says.

The biggest problem with this verse is the obvious fact that the Torah (the Law) does *not* say anything like this. In fact, our study of the Torah demonstrates quite the opposite. Women took an active and *outspoken* role in the community. They were expected to participate in synagogue worship and were free to do so at every level.

We know that Paul was a superior student of Scripture. As a Pharisee of the Pharisees, he undoubtedly memorized huge portions of Scripture, perhaps the entire Old Testament. One thing is certain. He knew the Law. He had no problem citing the Tanakh as the final authority on matters of faith and practice. His letters are full of Scriptural quotations. In fact, when he really wants to make a point, his usual practice is to say, "As it is written," followed by the Old Testament passage. But in this most crucial verse, Paul makes a huge "mistake". There is *no Scripture* at all that says women must be silent in the synagogue. Not one verse of the Law says anything like this. Furthermore, it is completely out of character for Paul to say, "as the Law says," and then *not* give the reference. This is nothing like Paul's normal writing. On this basis, Bilezikian suggests that this statement is not from Paul at all. How could it be? It doesn't sound like him. It doesn't read like him, and it has a serious flaw about the declaration of Scripture. Bilezikian believes that Paul is actually quoting the claim of his opposition. His opponents are telling the congregations that women should be silent, and Paul is reminding his readers of their bogus claim before he attacks their error. Unfortunately, many Christians don't realize what Paul is doing, and as a result, they misinterpret what he says. They start thinking that Paul is actually saying what his straw man is meant to say. Bilezikian offers further proof of this interpretation in the details of the Greek text. He makes a powerful argument, but even if you reject it, you must admit that this passage doesn't look anything like Paul's usual writing.

If we think that Paul actually issued this command, then we are faced with another serious problem. How can he enthusiastically endorse the verbal activity of tongues and prophecy with one breath and then tell women to shut up in the next? If there is anything we believe about God's Word, we believe it is not self-contradictory. If God inspired Paul to say that the whole congregation comes together and *all* speak in tongues (verse 23), then that same God cannot inspire the same author to tell half the congregation that they cannot open their mouths.

This very unusual command (if that's what it is) flies in the face of all that Paul says about *equality* under the Messiah. His watchword is "neither Jew nor Greek, male nor female." This theme is so strong in Pauline theology that one would have to conclude that Paul was schizophrenic to suggest that we are all equal, but women are a little less equal.

Bilezikian also points out that the word "all" here is uncharacteristic of Paul. The proclamation to *all* the churches doesn't fit the way Paul writes to individual church issues. The command for silence doesn't fit Paul's previous remarks. The appeal to Torah certainly isn't Pauline, since he would have known there are no such commands in Torah.

We know that Paul fully endorses the Tanakh. He refers to the Hebrew Scriptures again and again as his final source of truth. We also know that the Tanakh paints a picture of women as active participants at all levels of Hebrew society. They are not only mothers; they are judges, rulers, priestesses, leaders, guides, prophetesses, organizers, directors, teachers and *talmiydim*. Let's be direct about this. In the Old Testament, women speak out. It is hardly reasonable to suggest that Paul would override all Scripture, ignoring both God's design and Israel's history, in order to establish a contrary ruling. The traditional restrictive interpretation of Paul's words can only be proffered if we draw a hard and fast distinction between the Hebrew Scripture and the culture of Israel on one side and the new "Christian" religion on the other. But we have already seen that such a distinction is untenable, both theologically and historically. The bottom line is this: Paul speaks to particular issues. He is not making a general ruling here. He is not inconsistent with his own heritage and religious beliefs. Women in Paul's Scriptural heritage and in his personal experience take whatever role God directs them to take.

Most discussions about the role of women in ministry are really not about the opportunity women have to serve the Body. The real argument is about *authority*. No one debates the fact that women have always been included in God's redemptive plan. No one argues that women are clearly seen as financial underwriters, contributing members, socially conscious spokespersons or family educators. The real argument surfaces when the question is asked, "What authority do women have?"

Women of Authority

When we look carefully at the rest of Paul's letters, we find his commendation and recognition of women in roles of authority. Consider his final greetings in Romans 16. First, Paul names Phoebe, calling her a *diakonon* of the *ekklesia* (verse 1). Clearly Phoebe held a position of some distinction since Paul doesn't name a singe male in this role. There can be little doubt of the high regard he holds for Priscilla (verse 3), naming her before Aquila and designating her a "fellow-worker" in the Lord. We should note that *all* the congregations of the Gentiles are instructed to give her thanks for her efforts. One congregation meets in her house. In verse

6 Paul mentions another woman, Mary, acknowledging her exemplary status. Finally, verse 7 recognizes Junia as outstanding among the apostles.

This last verse also demonstrates how much theological prejudice has infected our translations. In the Greek text of Paul's letter, Paul names a couple, Andronicus and Junia (that's right, Junia, not Junias) as exemplary fellow-laborers for the gospel. This person's name is *'Iounia*, or in English "Junia," a woman. In other words, Paul is recognizing a couple where both the man and the woman are "outstanding among the apostles." In fact, according to Paul, they were believers before him, probably indicating that they were Greek proselytes and Messianic believers in the early assembly in Jerusalem.

In addition, the grammar of the phrase "outstanding among the apostles" can only be understood to mean that Junia was an apostle, not that she was known by the apostles. This would at least imply that Junia, a woman, was commissioned by the early church as "one sent" to carry the message of the Christ to the pagan world. There can hardly be a stronger endorsement for commissioned authority. We certainly know that there were more people considered apostles than the original twelve. Chrysostom (one of the earliest theologians of the church) recognizes Junia as an apostle. In spite of the contemporary translations decisions to make this woman's name into a man's name, the Greek won't allow it. Neither will the evidence from history.

Why is this important? Because if Junia, a woman, is an apostle, then it hardly makes any sense to claim that women in the early church were not allowed to teach or preach or be leaders. What else does an *apostle* do?

How can we possibly understand Paul's positive acclaim for Junia if Paul instructs all women are to be silent in all churches? The propagation of the idea that women are to be segregated to roles different than men flies in the face of biblical teaching, including Pauline teaching. It is inconsistent with equality under Christ; it ignores the Hebrew role of the *'ezer* and it is in opposition to the interpretation of the church fathers. Church tradition after 250 AD invented this misogynist idea. It's time to get rid of it. Translations of the text that propagate this bias verge on heresy. They reveal the misogyny of the translators, not the intent of the Most High God.

We might also mention Acts 21:9-10 naming the four daughters of Philip the evangelist. They were prophetesses. It seems contradictory to imagine that these four women, daughters of a man who is recognized as spreading the good news of the Messiah, were *silent* prophetesses. There is no indication whatsoever that Paul has any disagreement with their role in the congregation.

Paul's guidance to Timothy continues with a character description of the attributes of one who acts in the capacity of an "overseer" of the community. Paul begins the list with the phrase "if any man aspires to the office."[26] It seems clear from the translation that this office is open *only* to men. However, the Greek text is not as definite, using an expression that literally means, "if anyone."[27] Translators alter the neutral expression to "if any *man*" because they reason that the following condition, "a husband of one wife," logically implies that

---

[26] 1 Timothy 3:1
[27] The Greek is *ei tis*, commonly translated, "if any" or "if some." It is gender neutral.

the reference in the first part of the statement must be to males. According to the Greek text, it would be just as legitimate to argue that Paul was saying anyone could be an overseer but if that person is a male, he must have only one wife. Someone might argue that the rest of the passage couches these characteristics in terms of the male ("his" household, "his" children), but the Greek text does not allow this luxury. Paul continues to use the gender-neutral expression *ei tis* in connection with "house" and leaves the parental gender completely unspecified when it comes to children. In fact, the text only specifies the gender of the subject when Paul describes the potential pitfalls, and even there the only reason to add "he" or "him" is because the verb is a third person conjugation. It could just as easily be read "she" or "her."

We can reasonably conclude that Paul recognized the legitimate role of women as teachers, apostles, leaders, vocal practitioners within the congregation, administrators, prophetesses and fully active participants in the affairs and dynamics of society. There is nothing in the Greek text that *demands* otherwise. In addition, Paul would be contradicting Scripture to assert women were not allowed to take any one or more of these roles. Paul is *not* theologically illogical or forgetful. The only position consistent with the full range of his Torah commitment is the unrestricted participation of women in every role except that of the Levitical priesthood (which, of course, God Himself limited to certain males).

When we look across the *entire* scope of the Biblical record, we see God moving through men and women alike. We see that He chooses men and women as He pleases, to meet His purposes. We see that He makes little if any distinction between genders, given the cultural aspects of His election of the nation of Israel and its patriarchal society. We also see that God often, spectacularly, countermands this cultural bias and does things with women that only God could have imagined to do. Then we are impressed by the *original* choice that God made when He created Woman. He designed the *'ezer kenegdo*, not simply a helper and companion, but rather one who was to take on the role of sustainer, provider, protector and spiritual-awareness guide. If you will, God chose to use the woman as a symbol of His own role with regard to the human race.

What conclusion can we draw? Simply that God can do what He wishes to do, and we are not empowered to override His choices. Within the Body, God assigns every believer a role to play for the edification of the Body and the glorification of the Father. While we may use Scripture in a "checks and balances" process, we cannot deny God's sovereign choice. He is a God of surprises. The very fact that He would choose a virgin teenager to bear His Son is enough for us to see that He will constantly confound our expectations. We must be on the lookout for what is of Him, for Him and through Him. When we see it, we must acknowledge it – and adjust accordingly. Given what we have already seen in the history of God's revelation to men, we should not be surprised to find women in every role within the Body. In fact, we should be startled if this were not the case.

CHAPTER 13: Marriage

Submission

Having established that neither the Tanakh nor the writings of the apostles relegate women to limited participation in the Body or in society, it's time to conclude our study with a look at Paul's infamous statements about marriage.

We will consider the following passages:

Ephesians 5:21-33	Submission and headship
1 Corinthians 7: 1-5	Sexual relations in marriage
1 Corinthians 7:10-16	Marriage and non-believers
2 Corinthians 6:14	Unequally yoked
1 Corinthians 7:7-9	Staying single

Of course, now we can confidently analyze these passages from the perspective of Torah compatibility and rabbinic interpretation. What we find changes the usual understanding of Paul's words.

We may admit (perhaps reluctantly) that the teaching of the Church has not been in line with Scripture. We may admit that women can and do play significant roles in the believing community. We may acknowledge that the Tanakh supplies us with numerous examples of women in leadership roles. We may acknowledge that Jesus Himself treated women with dignity, respect and honor. We may conclude that Paul's comments to Timothy and the Corinthian congregation are the results of cultural circumstances and rabbinic understanding. But what about *submission*? Doesn't Paul (and Peter) make it abundantly clear that wives are to be in *submission* to their husbands? How can we reconcile the role of the *'ezer kenegdo* with Paul's clear pronouncement that "the man is the head of the woman."[28]

For the moment, put aside the accumulated cultural interpretation of this passage and reflect on the general theme of the Scripture. Ask yourself what we learned from the Genesis account. After all, Yeshua (Jesus) cites Genesis 2:24 as the authoritative text on marriage and that text clearly suggests that the male detaches himself from previous protectors and providers and attaches himself exclusively to a new *'ezer*. Properly understood, marriage is God's sacramental symbol of our covenant relationship and obligation to Him. How do these verbs apply to the common teaching that the husband is the head of the home?

Head of the Home

The role of the husband has often been interpreted in terms of the spiritual leader and decision-maker. Of course, in a Christian household, the first order of business is the spiritual condition of the marriage and that entails the full submission of the husband to his Lord and Savior. The covenant relationship that he enjoys with his Lord is to be transferred in like manner to the covenant relationship with his wife. This requires complete loyalty, fidelity and exclusivity. Our study of the Hebrew background leads us to this conclusion: God makes a covenant with Himself and all Mankind is blessed. God makes a covenant with Adam and the earth is blessed. God makes a covenant with Havvah and Adam is blessed. Now let's apply this conclusion to the issue of authority in the home.

---

[28] 1 Corinthians 11:3

Since Paul suggests that the husband is the "head" of the wife, we are inclined to imagine some sort of hierarchy of authority. Our cultural experience lends support to this hierarchical view. In the broken world, power plays a crucial role in relationship management. But with the covenant imagery in mind, what can we really say about this supposed hierarchy? Is it as power-conscious as we customarily believe? Or is the covenant relationship pointing in another direction?

The key to understanding the biblical view of mutual submission as opposed to the cultural view of submission of the wife is found in the difference between authority and control. One reason why we react so strongly to the Pauline claim that the husband is the "head" of the wife is based in the confusion of authority and control. We read Paul's remark about headship as if it were about control. But Greek clearly distinguishes between control and authority. In Greek, the word *dynamis*, from which we derive *dynamic*, *dynamo* and *dynamite*, is a word about power, strength and force. These three elements are fundamental to leadership by law (*de jure*), implying that the prescribed behavior occurs under threat of punishment. With regard to human interactions, *dynamis* is relationship *independent*. It makes no difference if I have a personal relationship with the police. I am still compelled to obey even if I don't know a single thing about the policeman. Relationships based on *dynamis* are, therefore, relationships of compliance, and, as such, have no more compelling motivation than the force used to insure performance. This is why any ethics based on compliance alone fails. As soon as the perceived threat is removed, there is no deeper reason to act accordingly. Consequently, human interactions based on *dynamis* are the most shallow of all relationships. They are "command and control" relationships, focused entirely on outward motivation (and punishment). Any marriage operating on this kind of basis will be nothing more than a master-slave arrangement. It will not qualify as a biblical marriage.

The fact that the husband has any authority at all exists only because the wife recognizes two critical things: first, she bestows upon her husband the right to act as the representative of the marriage covenant and secondly, she recognizes that it is in her own best interests to submit. It is *her voluntary submission* that bestows authority upon him. He does not have it as a "divine right of kings." He has it because *she grants it to him*.

Genesis 2:24 illustrates the proper model in the origin of marriage. A man *volunteers* to leave his previous protector and provider and give unwavering loyalty to his *'ezer*. The implication is that a man enters into covenant relationship with his wife because he acknowledges this is his duty in marriage. When he acknowledges her role as *'ezer*, he vouches that *it is in his best interests to do so*. What else could explain the radical shift in relationship dynamics in a patriarchal society? How else can we explain the fact that it is the *man*, not the woman, who breaks one relationship to establish another? Submission is all about loyalty. Genesis 2:24 makes it clear that the biblical paradigm example of *submission* within the context of a human covenant is marriage and it is the *man* who initiates it.

The statements of Paul and Peter cannot be dislodged from the dynamics of the covenant context of biblical history. There is no "law" in Christian relationship except the law of self-sacrifice *agape* love. God did not make husbands the policemen of marriages. He provided a way for a husband to exhibit the godly characteristics of humility, exclusivity and compassion. He provided an opportunity for the husband to give himself away, to *volunteer* to act like His Son.

This direction is confirmed by a careful reading of the often-quoted text in Ephesians 5:22 ("Wives, to your own husbands, as to the Lord"). The Greek text lacks the verb "be subject" or "submit." The verb must be supplied from the association of this verse with the previous verse. Verse 21 reads, "and be subject to one another in the fear of Christ." The model of submission is not that of a master and slave, nor even a lord and his subjects. The model is the general principle of all Christian interaction – mutual submission. Under the banner of Yeshua, *hupotasso* (submit) cannot be removed from *allelon* (one another). *Hupotasso* means, "to place in order, to arrange, put in submission." In this context, it describes the *voluntary, continuous, placement of my will under the authority of another*. Notice that the command to wives in verse 21 (and to husbands as well) is not to submit to their husbands as lord, but rather to submit to the one and only Lord, and in so doing exhibit behavior toward their husbands that reflects this inner act of the will. There is good reason why the verse does not command submission to the husband without this intervening step. No man may act as ruler over his wife and still fulfill the general principle of *mutual* submission. Furthermore, Sha'ul's exhortation to wives to submit to the Lord and therefore act as blessings to their husbands is a direct reflection of the design of the *'ezer kenegdo*.

Our examination of the Genesis paradigm clearly shows that Adam actually *relinquishes his decision-making* to

Havvah. This is implied by his excuse for his disobedience. The Genesis account also makes it clear that Havvah is uniquely equipped to act as spiritual guide in the relationship. Rabbi Sha'ul offers commentary on this Genesis account for the context of the Messianic community. He recognizes that submission is not about "who's in charge." It's about the willingness to relinquish personal agendas for the benefit of another. Paul calls upon wives and husbands to voluntarily relinquish their own agendas to the Lord and in so doing discover the freedom of mutual care for each other. In other words, Paul reiterates in New Testament terms the same Genesis idea of mutual *benefit*. It is the purpose of the *'ezer kenegdo* to benefit her husband. She accomplishes this purpose by relinquishing her will to the Lord in order to act as *'ezer* for her man. She gives up her own agenda in order to fulfill her covenant commitment to take responsible care of her mate. It is the purpose of the husband to sacrifice his agenda for his bride in order that he may model the sacrificial love of Yeshua for God's people. He gives up his own agenda in order that he may model the compassion, care and concern of the Father for his mate.

In the Greek text, the imperative incorporates a strong sense of exclusivity. "Be subject to your *own* husbands" reinforces the fact that Christian marriage is to exemplify the covenant relationship between God and His chosen. Husbands by virtue of their submissive act *belong* to their wives. Wives by virtue of their submissive act take ownership responsibility for their husbands.

Paul first declares the general principle: mutual submission (verse 21). He then provides an example of the practical application of this principle in the most intimate of human relationships: marriage. The behavioral characteristics of mutual submission are seen in both parties. For the wife, this is demonstrated in submission to Christ with resulting benefit exhibited toward her husband. For the husband, this is demonstrated in love for his Lord in the same manner that Yeshua loved the church, with resulting benefit for his wife.

Submission For Husbands

At this point, we need to take a look at Paul's exhortation to husbands. In Colossians 3:19 he says, *"Husbands, love your wives, and do not be embittered against them."* We know this is not just "feel good" love. Of course, love between a husband and a wife should feel good, but what Paul has in mind is love that gives up its own agenda for the benefit of the other. This is *agape* love – benevolence toward another at cost to myself. Since the relationship is *mutually* beneficial, loving my wife is really a good thing for me too. Sha'ul cautions against bitterness and the chaos it brings because acting according to the character of the Father *isn't easy*. A man must put aside most of his worldly training about being the boss, being tough and being in charge. His personal agendas must be put on the shelf. He relinquishes his desires in favor of hers. He steps out of the way in order to let her be all God designed her to be, trusting that God's directions to his *'ezer kenegdo* will bring him closer to God's purposes. He lets her be his blessing. But – it isn't easy! This process grates against everything the world expects and teaches. The temptation of bitterness hangs around the door, waiting for a chance to stick a foot in. Many men *concede* authority to their wives rather than joyfully supporting them. There is an enormous difference – a difference that can only be remedied in a heart-to-heart confession to the Lord. God's character, not hers, is impugned by this behavior. Perhaps that's why Paul is so direct. Don't let bitterness get under your skin. If serving your wife isn't joyful, go ask *the Father* what's wrong with your attitude.

Sha'ul concludes his discussion in Ephesians by saying, "Because the husband is the head of the wife." It appears that Paul is establishing a hierarchy of power. But is this true? The problem in translation is the misapplication of the meaning of "head."

Bilezikian's analysis of the translated term "head" significantly alters our culturally based teaching about a gender hierarchy. He conclusively demonstrates that the term "head" (*kephale* in Greek) is used as "source," not hierarchical authority. We have a similar meaning when we talk about the "head" of a river. In Hebrew, the comparable term *rosh* is found in the expression Rosh Hashanah, the "head" of the year. In an exhaustive review of every instance of *kephale* in the LXX, classical Greek literature and the New Testament letters, Bilezikian demonstrates there are no instances where *kephale* must be understood as hierarchical authority. He concludes:

> The use of "head" within the contexts where it is found in 1 Corinthians, Ephesians, and Colossians forces on us the conclusion that the concept of headship in the New Testament refers to the function of Christ as the fountainhead of life and growth and to His servant role of provider and sustainer. The New Testament contains no text where Christ's headship of the

church connotes a relationship of authority. Likewise, the New Testament contains no text where a husband's headship to his wife connotes a relationship of authority.[29]

In primeval history, God creates Adam. From Adam, God builds Havvah. The priority of creation allows Paul to argue that Man (the *adam*) is the *direct* reflection of God but woman is the *indirect* reflection. He is able to make this argument based on the *source* of the creation of man and woman. This is the sense Paul uses when he speaks of the husband as the "head" of the wife. The Man is the *source* of the Woman. God used the raw materials of the earth to create a man, but He used the raw materials of a man to make a woman. We saw just how important this pattern is when we examined the "measure for measure" description God gave after the first act of disobedience. In each case, the *source* became resistant to demonstrating the divinely ordered task. However, nothing about being the *source* implies hierarchical authority. The purpose of the source is *mutual reciprocity of benefit*. For men and women, this is egalitarian interdependence. Sha'ul's rabbinic application of the source (origin) of man and woman does not violate his prior Torah commitment to the purpose and honored status of the *'ezer kenegdo* just as his comments about Adam do not overturn the connection between Adam and the *'adamah*.

Someone may object that without a "final" authority, decisions can't be made. Someone has to make the tough choices when husband and wife disagree. Most men argue they must be the ones to call the shots when there is conflict. The real answer to this all-to-familiar

---

[29] Bilezikian, *Beyond Sex Roles*, pp. 248-249.

problem is: "Why?" Why must one take precedence over the other? If unity is the ultimate goal, if harmony is the final display of the true covenant marriage, why are we so anxious to get to a decision? What would happen if we decided *together* that we would do nothing unless *both* agreed? Under the umbrella of *mutual* submission, wouldn't that mean that I set aside my agenda in the favor of my spouse – and she would do the same? Where is the biblical suggestion that *any* marital decision comes about through compulsion or demand?

Genesis 2:24 contains a further hint. The Hebrew word for flesh is *basar*. The intentional reunification and harmony implied in this verse goes far beyond the physical act of sex. We see a hint at the deeper meanings here when we consider the homophone of *basar* (flesh). Genesis 2:24 proclaims the objective of reunion is "one flesh." Too often we think of this only in sexual terms, but it is far more than that. *Basar* has a homophone that means "publish, preach, or to bring news". Apparently, the Creator designed the "one flesh" for the purposes of publishing, preaching, and physically bringing His message to others. If we thought of this only in terms of our ability to communicate with the physical world, then our message might be about God's creative work in us. But marriage takes this imagery one step further. In marriage, our flesh becomes one. In terms of proclamation (*basar*), the union of husband and wife declares the unity of God. The meaningful deed of union in marriage reflects the image of God in Man. God is one. This fundamental tenet of Judaism can be seen here, in the discussion of the physical connection of sexual union. Marriage is God's unification proclamation. It is designed to display harmony inside the marriage in the outward manifestation of *one* flesh. Marriage is supposed to be the incarnation of *shalom* in human form. Seen from the outside, it is the billboard of God's unity. This is the goal of marriage – becoming one flesh. It is the voluntary *reunion* of submitted partners to inner and outer *shalom* as a primary display of God's glory. The *basar* of marriage reflects the unity of the Creator.

Sex in Marriage

Sha'ul's extended discussion of sex in marriage is found in 1 Corinthians 7:1-6. One principle governs the entire passage: each person in the covenant relationship of marriage exists for the benefit of the other. By now we know that this principle is firmly established in the Genesis account. Instead of directing the attention of the reader toward submission, Paul now speaks of authority, but his remarks are exactly the opposite of our normal expectations. A wife does *not* have authority over her own body. A husband does *not* have authority over his own body. Why? Because the authority belongs to the partner. We should have expected no less, given the metaphors in the Tanakh. Personal agendas, including sexual intimacy, are mutually submitted to each other. Ownership is given away. Responsibility for the well-being of the other person replaces demand for personal fulfillment, even when it comes to sex. Sha'ul is quite clear about this. "Stop depriving one another!"

Of course, men may be tempted to use this directive to *demand* sexual relations. And women may retreat from such bold language in fear of domination. Both reactions miss the point. My body does not belong to me. It belongs to my partner. The underlying assumption here is that I will treat your body with the same care, respect and honor that I would treat my own. Paul's remarks cannot be taken out of the context of his insight that the body is the temple of the Holy Spirit. Tenderness is the word of the day.

It's important to remember that the Hebrew idea of the body does not follow the Greek metaphysical separation of the human being into body, mind and soul. In Hebrew thought, we are embodied persons. We are fully homogenized instantiations of the divine image in the world. In other words, when Paul speaks about the ownership of the body, he is not talking about the spouse's authority over the *physical* structure. He is using a Greek word (*soma*) for a Hebrew concept (*nephesh*) to capture the idea of the *whole person*. This, of course, is exactly what we discovered in the analysis of ownership in the Song of Songs. Once again, Sha'ul is entirely consistent with the Tanakh.

Paul recognizes the power of sex. It is the most immediate physical method of reunification. But it is more than that. Sex completes the world of one. Therefore, it carries a frightening power. Because it has such incredible power, it almost cannot be trusted to its owner. It must be given to another for safekeeping and use. This is Paul's advice. The power of sexual energy is beyond (almost) human control, particularly the control of the one whose sexual desires are in full bloom. The danger is releasing this power while it is still in the hands of the one captured by desire. Unlike other desires that may be satisfied upon completion, sex knows no boundaries capable of being maintained by human agents. It must be given into the hands of someone else if it is to be used to bring unity. Therefore, my body must be handed over to my lover. It is far too powerful for me to own.

Paul's message here is about the methodology of blessing in the context of desire. While passion is a part of God's creation of the divine image, God intends passion to be *domesticated* by an act of submission. In the case of marriage, sexual desire is domesticated when it is delivered as a gift into the hands of the spouse. It is to be treated as a particularly special gift, a precious offering of the deepest need for intimate connection, but once it is given and domesticated, it is not to be repossessed. Song of Songs clearly demonstrates that the ultimate satisfaction in sexual union comes from relinquishing ownership to my lover.

But I'm Single

What about those who are not married? Paul comments, *"But I say to the unmarried and to widows that it is good for them if they remain even as I"* (1 Corinthians 7:8). A single person today stands between two worldviews. The culture tells us that we need to be married (or in some sort of "committed" relationship). For decades we've heard that fulfillment comes with coupling. The church teaches much the same thing. We are swayed by the bridal advertisements, the sit-coms and the constant bantering about the "twenty-nine areas of compatibility." We think that without someone special, we are destined for a life of less than real happiness. Worry takes over. Then we go about engineering our own partnership.

This is a Greek alternative. The world is filled with it. It begins with the fear that I will be alone. It ends with *making* things work out for me. There is another way. It is the way that places my agendas for living on the altar, watching them burn away. Leviticus informs me that what is consumed on God's altar is holy to Him.

Therefore I know that this deliberate act of self-denial is within His will. By the way, it isn't any different for someone who is married. If I am married *with an agenda*, I too am called to self-sacrifice. No person, married or single, can take this step *unless* that person first understands why there is no reason to be afraid. In this world, fear of the unknown is a powerful influence behind taking life in my own hands. But it is not the biblical way.

The God of the Bible is the sovereign King of the universe. When I commit myself to Him, I give Him the authority to decide these crucial life issues for me. I know that His plan is a good one. I know that He is perfectly capable of engineering my life so that I encounter (not find!) the right partner. And I know that if I do not encounter a partner, God is still good and His plan is still perfect. I have a choice to make here. I can languish in disappointment because I fear the unknown and I have adopted the partnership goal of the world, or I can wait expectantly for my Master and King to provide for me according to His purposes. I serve Him. He will never give me less than what I need to be able to fulfill His design for me. I can be confident in that. What I cannot do is focus my eyes on anything less than His character in actions. My Father who knows exactly what I need. In a way, those who are single are immeasurably blessed. Yes, I know it doesn't feel like that (after all, who am I to talk?). But God's standards are upside-down. I know that He never allows us to bear more than we can while we are upholding His honor. That means God knows who can be trusted to carry the extra loads and who can't be trusted to do so. The disciples called it being worthy to suffer for His name, and they rejoiced over His choices.

Here's the backwards part. We think that marital bliss is what makes us whole. God knows that some of us can actually better fulfill His purposes by not being married and He counts our willingness to go against the grain as something special. In fact, it is so special that few are called to such a life. Those who are called exhibit a devotion to Him that most of us mere mortals can't handle very well. To be single in this world is definitely upside-down; but upside-down is a mark of spiritual strength, not weakness. Don't be discouraged. The culture pushes the ordinary understanding of life's objectives. We who are followers of the King must leave those choices to Him. We don't run after the same goals. We let Him arrange life for us. And when He engineers being alone with Him, we can rejoice and relax. Life lived for Him is the best reward.

Applying The Teaching

What can we conclude about the New Testament commentary on our Torah paradigm? We can draw the following practical consequences:

1. The wife *grants* authority to the husband and voluntarily submits to him knowing that it is in her best interests to do so BECAUSE the husband sacrifices his own interest in order to offer all that he is for her well-being. Both of these acts of self-denial model the character of God. Both are demonstrations of the principle of mutual *blessing* designed into the fabric of being human.

2. The wife treats her husband as her exclusive property, taking ownership of his welfare BECAUSE he woos her with a compelling and unconditional love.

3. The wife responds to her husband with active obedience BECAUSE the husband honors his wife with unwavering faithfulness, fidelity and equality.

4. The wife maintains a life of purity BECAUSE the husband demonstrates complete dedication to the purpose of their unity, that they may be reunited as one (a unity of person) as an exhibit of the unity of God.

5. The wife honors and respects her husband BECAUSE the husband maintains absolute trustworthiness in behavior and purpose toward her.

6. The wife expresses thanksgiving and gratitude BECAUSE the husband demonstrates a life of continuous forgiveness, mercy and grace. Both demonstrate God's actions toward each other in the process of becoming human.

7. And BOTH exhibit submission to each other as to the Lord.

In conclusion, we see that the relationship between husband and wife is complex but clear. From a biblical perspective, the wife is designed to be the protector, provider, nourisher and guide. The husband is intended to relinquish previous dependencies and commit his entire sense of well-being into the hands of his *'ezer*. It is his responsibility to remember the God who made him and dedicate himself to the well-being of the one who came from him. Sin has disrupted this process, but it has not erased it. Wives still feel the intuitive and innate impulse to provide, protect and guide. Husbands still feel the need for care. The spiritual design of human beings equips us to recognize both roles as reflections of their common source in God. The Bible portrays redeemed marriage as a return to the *original* plan. But the Bible recognizes the reality of the fallen world, and, as a result, adds cautions to the redemptive call to action.

The wife must bring her innate design under the banner of submission – an act that portrays the heart of God more than any other. This is power relinquished, not grasped, modeling the *submission* of the Son. While she maintains theological and teleological ownership, she discovers that the responsibility of ownership involves unwavering service and unmitigated humility. Contrary to the ways of the world, her ownership is exemplified in her willingness to let go of control. She embraces the most difficult of all spiritual virtues: assumed responsibility without compelling authority. She lives for the *benefit* of her husband. In her walk with God, she blesses her husband.

The husband who is the recipient of this act of submission is cautioned to accept his role as one who is *granted* authority by another. He is a titular leader of the marriage only insofar as she is a follower. His position depends entirely upon his continuous effort to sustain her well-being. His authority is granted to him by mutual submission as he empties himself of his own agenda and takes up what is of value for her. He complements his wife's spiritual virtue by offering her *shalom* (well-being) without demanding reciprocity. He lives for her benefit. His is not power assumed or even power anxiously accepted. It is not power at all. It is sacrifice for the good of another. He is the *reluctant* leader. She offers him the opportunity to accept the role of servant, modeling his Master. She offers him the opportunity to demonstrate true humility; a word that entails *domesticated* power, power that has been brought under control.

The duet is complete. She takes responsibility for his life, but submits her will to the Lord's leading for his benefit. He accepts the role granted by her but turns all his efforts toward her well-being just as Yeshua sacrificed Himself for God's people.

Since this duet is played in the world as it is, biblical marriage must restore the elements of the redeemed world to a fallen universe. This is not the effort of two individuals but rather of a single unit. This is what it means to become one. And if God brings these together, who can ever separate them?

To be a unified whole (*nephesh hayah*) is to reunite the two that have been separated – to bring *us* back together – inside and outside. For men, becoming one flesh means loving my *'ezer kenegdo* for who she is, God's gift to me of a spiritual guide and relationship manager. For this reason, a husband places her well-being above all others. Well-being includes a lot more than just physical care and protection. Well-being includes emotional and spiritual wholeness, and for that to occur, husbands must honor the role of the *'ezer kenegdo*.

For women, becoming one flesh means taking ownership of their husbands. They place his well-being above all others by offering him all of who they are. A wife truly become **his** *'ezer kenegdo*. Wives were designed *to bless* their husbands. When a wife fulfills her God-designed role, every action she takes will be measured by the blessing it produces for her man. Just like God's blessings, these actions are not always pleasant, but they are always redemptive, always for the best purposes of the beneficiary.

Every husband wants the shelter of his wife's arms. Every wife wants the undying loyalty of her husband's heart. God designed it that way. It's up to us to live it.

CHAPTER 14: Aftermath Recovery

Now What?

What does an *'ezer* do today? How does a woman exercise her role as *'ezer* in the world *after* the Fall, a world where men make claims to be in charge and resist her design? And what does a husband do to acknowledge, encourage and support the role of the *'ezer* in a world that expects him to be the boss. The answers to these questions are actually distributed throughout Scripture if you look for them. Now that we know what God's *original* intention was in the design of the *'ezer*, we should expect to find *'ezer* actions displayed wherever God's redemptive activity reaches across the chasm created by the Fall. And when we look, that's what we see.

Consider the women that the Scripture designates as role models. They might not have the same prominence as men, but they are crucial nevertheless. Sarah, Rebekah, Rachel and Hagar come to mind. Isn't it interesting that the first woman after Genesis 3 to have a face-to-face encounter with God is an Egyptian slave? Isn't it important to note that this Egyptian slave woman is the first to give God a name? We could consider Miriam, Deborah, Ruth and Esther. We should certainly spend some time reading the love poetry of the *woman* who is the principal spokesperson in the Song of Songs. We could reflect on all those unnamed women who acted on behalf of the prophets. We certainly must include Hannah. Even the rabbis consider her prayer to be the epitome of true prayer before God. And how about the mother of Moses or the valiant woman of Proverbs 31?

After we catalogue the women of the Hebrew Scriptures, take a look at the women in the Apostolic writings. Look at their behavior, their courage, their daring, their unwavering support, their evangelism, their roles as teachers, apostles and prophetesses. Then think about the way that Yeshua interacted with women. His behavior is *the standard* for godly, responsible relationship in the redeemed community. Did He ever act with superiority over women? Did He ever diminish them, disparage them, refuse to include them, ignore them or act as though they had nothing of value to bring to the community? Of course not! In fact, one of the distinctive marks of Yeshua's ministry was the fact that He deliberately included women. Few rabbis of the first century would have done this. Mary and Martha both call Yeshua *Rabboni*. This is a term of deep emotional endearment, a way of expressing their devotion to a man who saw them according to God's original perspective. And, of course, there is Mary. Her response to the angel's announcement is a paradigm of submission to the will of God regardless of the consequences for her reputation, status and family honor. No man shows more devotion to the Lord than the woman, Mary.

Finally, we come to the remarks of Paul and Peter. Most of us have heard a sermon extolling the "God-ordained" hierarchy of men over women. Some of us have heard men teach that women have a restricted role in the redeemed community. Theologians carefully explain that this does not diminish the woman's *spiritual* standing before God. It simply delegates certain roles and positions to men. Now we see it isn't possible for Paul and Peter to do such violence to the Hebrew

Scriptures. Is it reasonable to conclude that these men, whose only "Bible" was the Old Testament, were so ignorant of the teaching found there that they could endorse anything except the vision of the redeemed community? Could they have missed the impact of God's design of the *'ezer*?

Let's be frank. Paul knew his "Bible" far better than you or I. He was a native Hebrew speaker. He was a Torah scholar. He probably *memorized* the entire Hebrew Scriptures. He spent three years under the personal instruction of the risen Lord. Is it reasonable to think that he would say things that contradict what the Hebrew Scriptures say? When we interpret Paul's letters or Peter's remarks *without* the foundation of the Hebrew Scripture, we are the ones who do violence to the text. There is simply no way that these men could have proposed or endorsed anything that was inconsistent with God's Word or God's character. We cannot understand the New Testament without first understanding the Old Testament. We need to be Hebrew thinkers before we can be Greek theologians.

Today you will have an opportunity to either act like an *'ezer* or allow an *'ezer* to play the role she was designed to perform. If you fail in your intended role, you do violence to God's design. If you fail, you endorse the broken world, not the redeemed community. It's up to you. Today is the day to be Hebrew about this.

Back To The Garden

Theological foundations are wonderful. Nothing is more important than alignment with God's design. But knowing the plan is different than carrying it out. We

Guardian Angel

may agree that our minds have been opened to the paradigm of the *'ezer kenegdo* and redeemed marriage, but the question remains: How do we make this happen? Marriage doesn't occur on paper. It takes place in the hard reality of human interaction. If redeemed marriage makes no difference in the kitchen or the bedroom, it is nothing more than another unattainable, ideal concept. Nice to know, but too hard to do.

What does this paradigm look like in action? What actually changes? Perhaps a few suggestions will get us moving in the right direction.[30]

> "Well I came upon a child of God
> He was walking along the road
> And I asked him, "Tell me where are you going"
> This he told me..."

1. Recognize who is with you. The one you share your life with is God's child and God's perfect gift to you. If you're the husband, then she is the perfect enemy. Perfect because God knew exactly why you needed this particular person and He provided her. Perfect *enemy* because only she is uniquely equipped to smooth your rough edges, to bring you face-to-face with your real destiny, to remind you to obey Him, to guide you toward deeper relationship, to lift you up when you need help and fence you in when you're out of bounds. If you're the wife, then your husband has been put into your care in order that he might do God's bidding. Your job is

---

[30] The following lyrics from Joni Mitchell, *Woodstock*, as sung by Crosby, Stills, Nash and Young

to take ownership to him so that everything you do helps him draw closer to his Lord. You have no other agenda than his *shalom*, just as he has not other agenda than the fulfillment of your true identity. Your support is unwavering. Your encouragement unfaltering. Your standards unbending. But it is never for you. The fruit of your life is food to his soul. You have met your partner and he is God's child too. So, you ask, "Where are we going – together?"

> "Well then can I walk beside you?
> I have come to lose the smog,
> And I feel myself a cog in somethin' turning.
>
> And maybe it's the time of year,
> Yes and maybe it's the time of man.
> And I don't know who I am,
> But life is for learning."

2. Remember it takes a *lifetime* to learn this new way. Patience, patience, patience. Don't be Adam. Forgiveness is the only thing that keeps us walking together. When forgiveness stops, so does the relationship. If God didn't forgive, we would never be able to know Him. The same is true with a spouse. If we are going to walk this road together, we will have to allow for missteps, stumbles and falls. No one does it perfectly. The more grace we supply to the marriage, the better chance we have to getting to the same place at the same time. This is *not* a race. The goal is to get there *together*. We won't know who we are if we arrive separately because God intended us to discover ourselves in one flesh. A house

divided cannot stand. And it can't journey very far either.

> "We are stardust, we are golden,
> We are caught in the devil's bargain
> And we got to get ourselves back to the garden"

3. The garden is the place of passion. The garden is delightful play. A redeemed marriage puts emphasis on both. It puts emphasis on the passion for each other and for God's billboard in one flesh. A redeemed marriage is playtime in the adventure of learning to love. God designed each spouse to be the source of sustaining delight for the other. Each partner's productive efforts should be nourishment for the other. No one lives in the garden of delight if he lives for himself. That was the serpent's suggestion. It's the devil's bargain. Neither husband nor wife can be a god. But together they can be a delight to themselves and to God. If our choices don't work for *both* of us, then they don't work. In practical application, unless there is mutual agreement, there is no agreement.

4. Redeemed marriage places the highest priority on devotion, not service. When Jesus corrected Martha's zeal by pointing out that Mary's devotion was of greater value, He gave us a clue about relationship maintenance. The husband (or wife) who proclaims, "But I do all this work for you," has confused service with devotion. Production, accumulation and achievement are not the equivalent of dedicated attachment and passionate intensity for your loved one. If they

were, all successful people would have satisfying marriages. What we intuitively know to be true is that the world's measurements of success have almost no bearing on the quality of marriage. But in the hustle and bustle of life, we excuse our lack of devotion by importing the false standards of the marketplace. More is not better. Redeemed marriages place time, affection and involvement far above property, power and performance. Whenever pressures from outside the marriage begin to dictate the values inside the marriage, we are on a trajectory away from God's design. What is true of our relationship with Him is also true of our relationships with each other. Intimacy demands attention. There is *no* substitute for time together. How do I do this? I set my sights on a daily dose of unexpected acts of devotion. I show my feelings in creative ways that break the routine. I think of fifty ways to keep my lover.

5. Redeemed marriages thrive with listening. If we truly want to know the will of God, we must *listen* to Him. When we come to God in constant prayers of petition, we presume that God is some kind of blessing machine. We might see Him as a God who exists to fulfill our wishes. Recognizing the lunacy of this approach causes us to confess our sinful presumption and begin to *listen* to His purposes. Precisely the same thing must occur in a redeemed marriage. Listening is far more important than talking. This is not the same as *hearing*. How many of us actually hone our listening skills (and attitudes) when it comes to spouses. The sweet rain of conversation eagerly

received transforms the marriage landscape into a field of exotic fragrances. In the garden, I listen to the sounds of God's creation. One of those is the *delight* of my spouse's words. Even if I have "intense fellowship,"[31] I never forget that the goal is to *bless* my spouse in whatever way I am able.

6. The hallmark of relationship with God is obedience. No disciple can claim intimacy with the Father or the Son and continue to disregard or disobey the instructions of the Lord.[32] John tells us quite plainly that such people are liars.[33] Certainly the same is true for the most intimate of all human relationships. Without obedience, there is no biblical marriage. But here is the sticking point: redeemed marriage does not focus on *your spouse's* obedience. It focuses on *your* obedience. In a redeemed marriage, we will not hear the complaint, "You didn't do what I asked." Instead we will often hear the apology, "I didn't do what you asked." In a redeemed marriage, obedience is never about *control*. Control shifts culpability to the behavior of the *other* person. Redeemed marriage places the emphasis on *my submission*, not *yours*. I live to bring *shalom* into your life. It is my failure that prevents your well-being, and so, obedience is always about me. The marriage analogy parallels the general principle of *mutual submission in the Lord*. I never have grounds for

---

[31] "Intense fellowship" is the wonderful description of Mrs. Arulampalam of Adelaide regarding arguments with her husband.
[32] Luke 6:46
[33] 1 John 2:4

questioning the obedience of Yeshua. His holiness is substantiated by the Father. The only one who has an obedience problem in relation to the Lord is me. Since I am to submit to the Lord as an act of marital fidelity, it follows that any issue of obedience originates with me, not with my partner. The first place I look when I think my spouse is not being obedient is at myself. What am I doing that is disrupting the harmony that naturally exhibits obedience? In other words, my spouse is a *mirror*, not a magnifying glass. Just imagine how things would have changed if Adam had adopted this principle.

7. Redeemed marriages reverse the cultural emphasis on the self. The greatest indulgence in the Western world is self. Everywhere we look, we are greeted by the constant encouragement to make ourselves the center of life. "Take time for yourself. You deserve it." "Live famously." "Be satisfied." "Find yourself!" One hundred and one mottos espouse the practice of "me first." A redeemed marriage looks at life from a different perspective. If Genesis 2:24 is the foundation of marriage, then there is no "me and you" in this covenant. There is only "us." Therefore, my identity is not found in what I do for myself but rather in what I do for you. I am "Rosanne's husband." That is what defines me. I become who I am by putting my spouse's well-being at the top of my priority list. In other words, *I practice the presence of my spouse*. Of course, we are quite aware of the typical spiritual priority: God, others, me. But I believe that this is not the order for those of us who wish to live redeemed

marriages. The passage in Ephesians gives us the correct order: The Lord, my spouse, us. There is no "*me*" in the equation at all.

8. Ownership is one of the fundamental themes of Scripture. The Bible unashamedly supports the idea of private ownership and supplies a legislative framework to protect it. Just as redeemed marriages reverse the cultural preoccupation with self, redeemed marriages take a different approach toward ownership. First, redeemed marriages recognize ownership is a *gift*, not a right. What God puts in my hands is not mine. It is His. I am steward over His property. Therefore, I am *not* free to do what I wish with it. I am free to exercise the authority of being His steward. This distinction is essential for redeemed marriage. It supports Paul's assertion that my body belongs to my spouse, not to me. My spouse exercises God's stewardship over my physical well-being. Of course, this is not the limit of stewardship, but it should be the most obvious. Ownership entrusts me with the care of the other. My responsibilities of ownership include all that is needed to insure that God's full intention is realized in the life of my spouse. There are no circumstances where I can justify my inaction on the basis of the other's choice. I am steward regardless of the other person's circumstances or behavior. So, I look after my spouse's physical, emotional, mental and spiritual peace and prosperity. Secondly, because redeemed marriage is a *mutual* covenant, I am also the recipient of my spouse's care for me. The

implication is clear: each person relinquishes the right of self-governance to the other and both parties take on the responsibility of the other's well-being. This pattern in marriage is exactly the same pattern in the Body. I am called to produce fruit from God's design in my life, but that fruit is not for my consumption. It is for the blessing of others. In marriage, I am called to be fruitful *for the sake of* my spouse.

9. Refusing interference and distraction is essential to intimacy with the Lord. It is just as essential to maintain the intimacy of a redeemed marriage. With little reflection, we will agree that life does it's best to pull us apart. Work, social obligations, even church activities can become thorns of discontent. But perhaps the greatest of all interruptions to intimacy in a redeemed marriage is children. There is no question that the roles and responsibilities parents have toward children are biblically supported. Nevertheless, a redeemed marriage must operate on the principle that spouse comes before child. As demanding as raising children truly is, nothing damages a marriage more than the substitution of the needs of children for the devotion to a spouse. The Bible makes the order of priorities clear. Mutual submission to the Lord followed by submission of the wife, sacrificial love of the husband and obedience of children. Notice that this order carries the *'ezer* undercurrent. First in human priority is "wives, submit." Second is "husbands, love." Only after these two do we find, "children, obey." Just as Adam's refusal to forgive sets the stage for a legacy of dysfunctional marriages, so Havvah's

decision to replace Adam's priority position sets the stage for a legacy of dysfunctional parenting.

10. One final word. Redeemed marriage is not a new authoritarianism. Just as there is no biblical support for the hierarchical authority of the husband, so there are no biblical grounds for a new hierarchy of the 'ezer. Husband and wife stand equally before the Lord. Our need for redemptive living is exactly the same. And we are created so that when we exercise the roles God intended, the fit is perfectly in line with planned divine harmony. The new Adam refuses to let a fallen world dictate his interaction with his wife. He lauds her as 'ezer kenegdo, tilling the soil so that she can develop her capacity and destiny. He clears away the thistles and thorns that prevent her from being what God designed her to be. His job is to provide the fertile ground for growth. The new "Eve" assumes the role lost to her predecessor by taking full responsibility as the steward-owner of the mate in her charge. She lives in obedience to her calling, relinquishing her desires in order to bring about the well-being of her partner.

One prepares the ground. One plants and cultivates. Both enjoy the harvest.

> "We are stardust, we are golden,
> We are caught in the devil's bargain
> And we got to get ourselves back to the garden"

Application Summary

God created an ordered existence. Man, as male and female, reflect that order. My life needs God's order.

Being human is a *verb,* not a noun. Just as God is known in the manifestation of His actions, so the creature that reflects God's image is manifest in action. Being human is being like the order-making God. My life needs to exhibit order-making in the world.

Man is an order-taker and an order-maker. Man, both male and female, expresses what it means to be human by doing what protects and continues life, in harmony with the will of the Creator. My unique sexuality equips me to perform one of these roles.

The "prime directive" is a description of the *acts that manifest* what it means to be human: to be fruitful, to increase, to act as God's regents, to steward the earth, to act with designated authority. I must work toward the prime directive.

Being human means acting in harmony with God's creation. Where my life exhibits or endorses chaos, disharmony or life threatening behavior, I must change.

Male and female are *equally* responsible and *equally* enabled to carry out this task. They are interdependent without an implicit hierarchy. At the most general level, there are no excuses for independent action or exclusion.

Human being is a process, not a state of existence. I am truly a work in progress.

Man as *male* is the one who is called to remember and to obey. He is designed to manifest thought as action. He is uniquely equipped to demonstrate faithfulness in word and deed as a reflection of God's character. If I am a man, I must know what God says and act on it.

Where there is no harmony in relationship, neither male nor female are manifesting human being. The first order of the business of being human is a thorough assessment of the level of harmony in life *together*.

I must evaluate my *actions* as the real measure of my humanity. I am a verb, a reflection of God's revelation as the verb "to be". In some fundamental sense, who I am is manifest in my behavior.

There is no hierarchy in God's original design. If I am acting as if there is, something is wrong with how I see the world.

Whether I am one who remembers or one who protects the boundaries, my uniqueness is a function of the role that I play in interdependence with each other.

I am human when I am in the dynamic of a relationship with God *and* with another. One without the other leaves something out of the necessary combination.

The man is the one who serves the earth and in the process nourishes his own substance. His service is his work and his work is a form of worship of the Creator who provided the earth from which he came.

The man is the one who was put in the place of God's delight and who is to delight in what God provides.

The man is the one who needs a guide and protector in order that he might work/worship the Creator and delight in His provision.

If I am a man, I am called to express my worship in work. That means I must be doing what delights God and blesses others. I am called to remember His instructions and obey them and to incorporate them in the community of "us". I am required to remember that the woman came from me, is equal to me and is necessary for me to fulfill what God has given me to do.

The woman is the last of creation, the final achievement of God's design, the capstone of His handiwork.

The woman is the one equipped for the assignment of protecting the boundaries of obedience.

The woman stands apart from the man as an extension of himself, to challenge, encourage, protect, nourish and rescue him. She is attuned to God by design, but not for herself. She lives in order that *he* might be obedient.

If I am a woman, I am part of God's covenant arrangement. I am designed to be aware of His moment-to-moment direction. As a women, I must know what God says and protect His word. By doing so, I am empowered to serve as a *benefit* to my husband.

God's design for marriage rests on this foundation. Where it isn't in place, the relationship falters. The *original* design is the way marriage is supposed to work. The closer we operate according to the original, the more aligned we will be with God's design.

Where there is no harmony in relationship, neither male nor female are manifesting human being. The first order of the business of being human is a thorough assessment of the level of harmony in life yoked *together*.

If I am a woman, I must evaluate my *actions* as the real measure of my humanity. I am a verb, a reflection of God's revelation as the verb "to be". In some fundamental sense, who I am is manifest in my behavior.

There is no hierarchy in God's original design. If I am acting as if there is, something is wrong with how I see the world.

Whether I am one who remembers or one who protects the boundaries, my uniqueness is a function of the role that I play in interdependence with each other.

I am human when I am in dynamic relationship with God *and* with another. One without the other leaves something out of the necessary combination.

If I feel alone in my marriage, a part of who I am is missing. That part is found in my spouse, not in anything else. I must recover it by allowing my spouse to be what God designed him or her to be.

Marriage depends on the faithfulness of the man and the double-facing empowerment of the woman. He sticks like glue no matter what. She faces him in protection and provision while she faces away from him in challenge and confrontation. A man *must* allow the *'ezer kenegdo* to live according to her design. A woman *must* encourage her mate to live according to his work/worship (*avodah*). In this way, the two become one.

The principle objective of marriage is to display the unity of God in the living reality of mutual interdependence.

God's original design of the *'ezer kenegdo* is the culminating masterpiece of creation, equal in every way with the man as a human being but uniquely gifted in her assignment.

She is to set the boundaries and guard them *for him*. She is to be his first line of defense, his spiritual guide, his protector and nourisher. She plays the role of God in the physical interaction on the human plane. She is exactly what he needs in order to be what God calls him to be.

Her greatest longing is to be his greatest defense. She is built for that and it will not be denied, even if the direction gets misplaced.

In God's perfect world, she takes ownership responsibility for her man, and he welcomes it because he knows she is uniquely designed to bring about what is best for him. She is ready and willing to set aside every other agenda in order to bless him with her care.

In the fallen world, she is still called to this unique and sacred task, and occasionally we see her accomplishing her role with such nobility, strength and skill that we extol her valor in songs of praise. We recognize this is the true goal of all women – to be valiant warriors for the men God has given them – and we realize this really is possible, even in a twisted world.

In the renewed and restored world, God will return to the original design and the woman will once again assume the full role she was intended to fulfill.

Therefore:

The wife treats her husband as her exclusive property, taking ownership of his welfare BECAUSE he woos her with a compelling and unconditional love.

The wife responds to her husband with active obedience BECAUSE the husband honors her with unwavering faithfulness, fidelity and equality.

The wife maintains a life of purity BECAUSE the husband demonstrates complete dedication to the purpose of their unity, that they may be reunited as one in body, mind and spirit.

The wife honors and respects her husband BECAUSE the husband maintains absolute trustworthiness in behavior and purpose toward her.

The wife expresses thanksgiving and gratitude BECAUSE the husband demonstrates a life of continuous forgiveness, mercy and grace.

The wife grants authority to the husband and voluntarily submits to him knowing that it is in her best interests to do so BECAUSE the husband sacrifices his own interest in order to offer all that he is for her well-being. Both of these acts of self-denial model the character of God.

The *'ezer kenegdo* is designed to be lost in God *in order that* she may fulfill her role with her spouse. She will be protector, provider, challenger and spiritual guide *in proportion to* her submission to her Creator.

A husband who prevents his wife from being lost in God, by whatever means, prevents her from being who she was designed to be. He suffers the consequences, finding himself alone at the depths of his being.

"A woman's heart should be so lost in God that a man must seek God to find her." Chris Wyatt

BE A BLESSING and BE BLESSED

Skip Moen is the author of

Words to Lead By

Spiritual Restoration Volume 1

Jesus Said to Her

God, Time and the Limits of Omniscience

and several thousand pages of daily explorations called *Today's Word*

All are available at:

skipmoen.com

Readers of *Today's Word* and members of *At God's Table* offer many blog comments about the Hebrew view of Scripture at this web site.

Made in the USA
Columbia, SC
04 August 2021